PENGUIN BOOKS

Chosen

'There is much that is intriguing here . . .
There are beautiful moments, as when Fraser's
youngest son is baptised in the River Jordan'
Rosamund Urwin, *Sunday Times*

'I spent all day reading this book, unable to stop. So
joyously eclectic, so bitingly honest, such a startling mingling
of the vulnerable with the intellectual, the search with
the homecoming. I cried, I laughed, and most of all I thought.
This is such an incredibly important and necessary book'
Michael Coren, author of *Epiphany: A Christian's
Change of Heart and Mind over Same-Sex Marriage*

'Interesting and accessible'
David Herman, *Prospect*

'A fascinating hybrid of past, present and future, Chosen
reflects Giles Fraser's astounding capacity for honesty,
turbocharged articulation and spiritual insight. He explains
beautifully the interweaving of Christianity and Judaism that
will resonate with many, and not just those from mixed
religious backgrounds. His scholarly explanations and personal
explorations brought me much wisdom. A tour de force'
Rabbi Laura Janner-Klausner

'A compelling account of a personal, religious, and philosophical
journey. Filled with humanity and wisdom, *Chosen* is a
riveting and rewarding read. Highly recommended'
Professor Quassim Cassam

ABOUT THE AUTHOR

Giles Fraser is Vicar of St Anne's, Kew. He has been a Lecturer in Philosophy and chaplain at Wadham College, Oxford, and Canon Chancellor of St Paul's Cathedral. He is the author of *Redeeming Nietzsche: On the Piety of Unbelief, How to Believe: Investigating Wittgenstein* and *Christianity with Attitude*. For some years he wrote the he wrote the 'Loose Canon' column in the *Guardian* and is a regular broadcaster on *The Moral Maze* and *Thought for the Day* on Radio 4.

GILES FRASER

Chosen

Lost and Found between
Christianity and Judaism

PENGUIN BOOKS

PENGUIN BOOKS

UK | USA | Canada | Ireland | Australia
India | New Zealand | South Africa

Penguin Books is part of the Penguin Random House group of companies
whose addresses can be found at global.penguinrandomhouse.com.

Penguin
Random House
UK

First published in Great Britain by Allen Lane 2021
This edition published in Penguin Books 2022
001

Typeset by Jouve (UK), Milton Keynes
Printed and bound in Great Britain by Clays Ltd, Elcograf S.p.A.

The authorized representative in the EEA is Penguin Random House Ireland,
Morrison Chambers, 32 Nassau Street, Dublin D02 YH68

A CIP catalogue record for this book is available from the British Library

ISBN: 978–0–141–97762–1

www.greenpenguin.co.uk

Contents

Preface   vii

Author's Note   xi

1 Justification   1

2 Resignation   25

3 Ghosts   51

4 Romans   93

5 Temple   134

6 Seven Blessings   179

7 The Sign of Jonah   206

Select Bibliography   217

Acknowledgements   219

Preface

This book is a ghost story. And, like many ghost stories, it follows a well-established pattern. The ghost arrives unexpectedly, taking advantage of a moment of weakness. It seems to carry a message, though its meaning is unclear and confusing. After much struggle the ghost is laid to rest. Peace is reclaimed. Yet nothing is quite the same again.

At the end of October 2011 I resigned from my dream job at St Paul's Cathedral. Early on in that eventful month the Occupy movement had set up a camp of tents within the curtilage of Christopher Wren's famous monument, the mother church of London. Some called for greater democracy in the City of London, some called for the overthrow of the global economic order, while others were looking for somewhere to sleep for the night. A large banner with the words 'What would Jesus do?' fluttered in the breeze. For a few weeks during the winter of 2011–2012, people were debating theology and capitalism down the pub and in the comments pages of newspapers. Was this a moment of change? Was capitalism beginning to fall apart?

It wasn't. The bailiffs came on the night of 25 February 2012. In a matter of hours, squads of police in riot helmets had cleared the camp and gathered together piles of tatty canvas into waiting rubbish trucks. Some protesters attempted to regroup in another part of the City, but most had already gone their separate ways. After four months of occupation, it was common for exhausted protesters to experience a complicated combination of relief and regret. And over the next few years, I kept in touch with several of them. Some fell into depression – the daily adrenaline of protest was followed by a period of soul-searching as many wondered what it had all been for. Some left the country to travel and find themselves. Some lives fell apart; others threw themselves into environmental protest – Occupy turned out to be something of a political nursery for Extinction Rebellion.

For me personally, the resignation from St Paul's triggered a period of considerable darkness. I suppose the right term is probably depression, though for some reason I remain reluctant to characterize it that way. I am ashamed to admit that I found the loss of status difficult to deal with, as I did the loss of direction. I struggled in the new parish. I drank too much. I pushed away those who had been closest to me. I didn't want to speak to my parents. My marriage of twenty years fell apart. Pain and hurt radiated out from my inner chaos.

It was at the bottom of this pit, just a few weeks after the Occupy protesters had been evicted, that something bizarre took place. The Germans have a great word for it: *unheimlich* – roughly translated, 'uncanny'. It came out of nowhere and felt so entirely disconnected from the events of the previous few months that for a long time I found it strangely difficult to speak about. These days I still tell people – partly to wind them up, but also semi-seriously – that I saw a ghost. Why not a ghost? After all, wasn't what happened to St Paul on the road to Damascus a little bit like seeing a ghost – the experience of something that won't stay buried, something both frightening and transformative? New Testament scholar Tom Wright, slightly disapprovingly, has called the road to Damascus experience 'a honey trap for psychological speculation'. But unlike him, I have found psychological speculation, and in particular a certain amount of Freud, a useful lens through which to wrest meaning from my own apparition.

What I saw wasn't a ghost, of course. Not a Scooby-doo ghost anyway. More Dickens perhaps. But ghost is still the closest characterization I can think of to capture the experience of that face peering out at me from a large oil painting hanging in the corner of a Liverpool synagogue. Unlike St Paul, mine wasn't a vision of the resurrected Jesus. It was of a very different Jew, a distant relative. This was the face of my great-grandfather's brother, Samuel, who ran the synagogue in Liverpool for over thirty years.

What follows is in part the story of a Jewish family that did their best to assimilate into this country. They climbed out of the backstreets, did well for themselves, sought out the establishment, changed their name from Friedeberg to Fraser, and finally changed their religion. I was the first ever non-Jew on my father's side. And I had become a priest at St Paul's Cathedral – as establishment and assimilated a position as it is possible to imagine. Samuel's gaze pierced my conscience, convicted me. I felt a fraud, as if something fundamental about my family had been lost, or betrayed. Perhaps Christianity was the final betrayal? Was this, deep down, why it didn't work out for me at St Paul's? Perhaps I just didn't fit in.

But this burgeoning fascination with all things Jewish inevitably meant that a whole load of questions about my Christianity started to pile up, which is why, despite the fact that this is on the face of it a memoir, there is a lot of theology too. My own slow emotional reconstruction became utterly inseparable from asking myself some very basic questions about the relationship between the faith that I had given my life to and the one my father had abandoned. Ever since St Augustine wrote his *Confessions* in the late fourth century, theology and memoir have had a remarkable affinity – one that has arguably been much damaged by the

ix

professionalization of theology as a discrete academic specialism. By contrast, the sort of theology I am interested in often works like blotting paper: it draws deeply from the personal, psychological, emotional and indeed the political circumstances of the writer. Hopefully, this book is informed by good scholarship. But it is not a work of scholarship. It is, I suppose, a rather peculiar sort of salvation story.

This journey felt – and still feels – ideologically perilous. To explore the interplay between Christianity and Judaism is to dig into a world of historic – and not so historic – pain and anger. Christianity is the original ideology of Jewish persecution and the earliest propagandist for antisemitism. Samuel Friedeberg pitched me into a world of questions I had been dodging all my life. Writing about them still scares me. But as I slowly got better, so a very different understanding of Jesus of Nazareth came into view. And with it came a very different life.

Author's Note

The translation of the Bible I tend to work from is the New Revised Standard Version (NRSV) and most quotations are taken from there. But there are times when other translations – the New International Version (NIV), for instance – are more helpful in bringing out a particular point, and in such circumstances I have used the most suitable alternatives.

1. Justification

For the good which I will, I do not; but the evil which
I will not, that I do . . . O wretched man that I am!
Who shall deliver me from the body of this death?

Romans 7:15, 24

I.

And then, towards the end of that long, sleepless night, surrounded by all the usual paraphernalia of introspective
misery – the spent promise of overflowing ashtrays and
chipped mugs stained with the muddy remains of cold black
coffee – I promised myself that I would write it all down. I
had got through that night, after all, and so I could get
through another. My study stank of last night's booze and of
sweaty-stale desperation. I had hardly moved from the chair
in hours, but my heart was still thrashing away in my chest. It
had been a near miss, and fear was expressing itself physically, in pulsing waves of nausea. I had stood too close to the
edge, peered too eagerly into the pit, reached out towards
that cheap absolution of total sleep where all things are forgotten but nothing is forgiven. I'm embarrassed to admit it
now. Ashamed. What if my children read this? But back then
I was drowning under thick black slime.

A few weeks before, I had loitered outside the rope shop
in Covent Garden like a furtive schoolboy outside a Soho sex
shop. The thought first began as an idle speculation, wafting

across my consciousness, easily dismissed. But it lingered. After a while it sat on me, beckoning, demanding attention. I would reassure myself that there was an ocean of distance between ideation and reality, that thinking about it and doing it were two totally different things. With this distinction in place, I gave myself too much permission mentally to experiment. I assumed the imagination could go as mad as it liked inside the machine, just so long as it wasn't allowed access to any of the levers of action. I should have known this was rubbish. I wasn't thinking straight. Mentally constructed scenarios entered more and more into reality. Practical details were considered. Possible venues were scoped out and paced about in. Plans were made. I had slowly, gradually, chipped away at the distance between thinking it and doing it.

Yes, I'm coy about it now, embarrassed even. And yet, back then I would repeat the word in my head, trying to acclimatize myself to the idea, to make friends with it. Odd as it may sound, the closer it came to fruition, the better I felt. It was as if I had finally found a way to do something about the darkness, to take some sort of action. Suddenly, there was a plan. I would obsess about the where and the how. I would think about what sort of knot to use and trawl the web for instructions on how to tie it – surprisingly difficult, as it turns out. When I did sleep, my dreams came straight out of a horror movie. I would think about the merits and difficulties of different venues: the strength of the banisters at home or whereabouts on the church balcony I could secure the rope. I didn't want to end up at the bottom of the stairs with just a broken leg. But where did I want to end up? And if I succeeded, what poor bugger, looking for their priest or their dad, would find me hanging from a rope, blue and bloated?

Surprisingly, the Hebrew Bible offers no clear-cut condemnation of suicide. It reports the suicides of Saul and Samson without a whiff of moral disapproval. Saul deliberately fell on his own sword because he had been defeated in battle by the Philistines. And Samson, again against the Philistines, killed himself in the world's first recorded suicide attack. Shackled against the vast pillars of the Philistine temple in Gaza, Samson forced apart these great load-bearing columns and deliberately brought down the roof – on himself and on the thousands of men, women and children worshipping underneath. As the book of Judges makes clear, Samson couldn't have carried out his 'martyrdom operation' had God not restored his superhuman strength. This doesn't look like a divine condemnation of Samson's suicide to me. It looks more like divine complicity, even approval.

Early Christianity also flirted with the approval of suicide. During the Roman persecution of the early Church, the celebration of those who willingly, even enthusiastically, gave up their lives for the faith was not easy to distinguish from a glamorization of deliberate self-destruction. In the early fourth century Bishop Eusebius, one of the Church's original propagandists, describes two sisters who drowned themselves rather than have their virginity taken forcibly by Roman soldiers. Being a martyr was a sure route to heaven and to posthumous celebrity. After all, did not Jesus go willingly to his death? Did he not choose it? Surely, he was given every opportunity to avoid it. So wasn't he also some sort of suicide?

Yet, despite all the ambiguity of this early enthusiasm for martyrdom, for Christians suicide was always going to be a bad thing when explicitly named because suicide was associated with Judas, the ultimate traitor. And, unlike the previous six suicides mentioned in the Hebrew Scriptures, all of which had some sort of wartime element, the Judas suicide was the only one we might call existential. After betraying Jesus to the Romans – and for money – he went away and hanged himself, sick with guilt and remorse. With this betrayal, Judas became the most hated man in Christian history, often depicted in medieval art as swinging from a rope. Judas came to represent a shameful suicide.

It was St Augustine who first argued that suicide contravened the sixth commandment: Thou shalt not murder. Later still, St Thomas Aquinas intensified the prohibition with the insistence that suicide was unpardonable. From the mid-sixteenth century onwards, those who took their own lives were denied a Christian burial. In England, suicide was declared a crime and those who killed themselves had their property confiscated by the crown. The bodies of suicides were physically attacked and dumped unceremoniously on rubbish tips.

Given that it was in and around the cold and lonely stones of St Paul's Cathedral that I began my slide into darkness, it was some comfort to discover that it was the Dean of St Paul's, the priest and poet John Donne, who first signalled a change in the Church's attitude to suicide. His 1608 essay, *Biothanatos*, encouraged 'a charitable interpretation of their Action, who dye so'. Donne stated that Jesus' death, in so far as it was voluntary, was also some sort of suicide. But anxious not to be misunderstood, he refused to allow these thoughts to be published. *Biothanatos* was probably not a cause but a consequence of changing attitudes. Sentiment and pastoral understanding began slowly to whittle away at the hard legalism of the Aquinas position. It wasn't until

1882 that the Church of England allowed suicides to be buried in consecrated ground, and only in 2017 that Church law was finally changed so that suicides were able to have the same funeral service as others – in reality, though, the Church had changed its teaching in practice long before it changed it in theory.

From the mid-eighteenth century onwards, and particularly with the advent of Romanticism, another problem presented itself: not a damnation of the suicide, but the glorification of the suicidal person as some sort of romantic hero. In 1774, Goethe published the literary sensation *The Sorrows of Young Werther*, the story of a painfully earnest young man, tortured by unrequited love, who ends up shooting himself. All over Europe, other young men started to dress up in yellow trousers and blue jackets, imitating Werther. They also began to imitate the manner of his death, and Goethe's book was banned in several countries. Suicide was discovered to be contagious, something that people copied. And so the roots of a poisonous connection between suicide and the romantic hero began to form at the very same time as the development of modern celebrity culture. These days suicide is the number-one cause of death of men under forty-five. The link between suicide and depth of feeling has become a terribly dangerous cliché. From Vincent van Gogh, to Virginia Woolf and, more recently, Kurt Cobain, there are now a growing number of famous suicides.

I had come across the insidious power of this connection a few months before I began my own descent into the darkness. In February 2010 the fashion designer Alexander McQueen hanged himself in a haze of cocaine and sleeping pills a few days after the death of his beloved mother. I was approached by a coterie of his giraffe-like model friends asking whether St Paul's Cathedral could be the venue for his memorial service. I put the case to my colleagues that McQueen clearly met the criteria for a service in the cathedral – he was a person of national significance and he had a strong local connection. And they accepted this.

But friends of Lee – as they knew him – and members of the fashion industry wanted something a great deal more than a straightforward memorial service; they wanted an extravaganza timed to coincide with London Fashion Week. At one planning meeting they asked for the service to end with pipers from the Scots Guards leading the congregation out of the cathedral; and for a snow machine to be erected on the top of the west end – because, said with a straight face: 'Lee loved the snow.' I said no.

Even without the snow, the service was quite some event, packed with fashionista royalty in their little black dresses and huge dark sunglasses. American *Vogue* editor Anna Wintour refused to read the lesson from the normal St Paul's lectern because it wasn't high enough. She wanted 'her people' to construct another one just for her, made to measure. Again, that was a no. It was obvious from Wintour's reaction that she was used to getting her own way. In the service itself, the singer Björk, in a costume of feathers and huge paper wings, sang 'Gloomy Sunday', also known as the 'Hungarian Suicide Song'. It was once banned by the BBC for being so sad that they believed it could encourage people to take their own lives.

The day after the funeral Peter Hitchens, columnist for the *Mail on Sunday*, phoned me up and we had a bad-tempered exchange. He argued that the service was celebrating suicide. I disagreed. Only later did I discover that this wasn't an academic matter for him. His mother had taken her own life, apparently in a suicide pact with a lapsed Anglican priest. I reacted strongly against Hitchens's complaint at the time. But looking back, I think he may have had a point.

During my twenty-five years as a priest, I have taken a number of funerals for people who have killed themselves. None of them made it into the papers or had such a glamorous cast of mourners as Alexander McQueen. Of course, McQueen had such mourners because he had a glamorous life – at least, publicly. But the romance and excitement masked a very different reality. The reason the aestheticization of suicide is such a treacherous lie is that it ignores the fact that most of the people who kill themselves are trapped and desperate – or just plain unwell. They may be suffering from depression or schizophrenia; or in debt, or homeless, or addicted to alcohol or drugs – or a combination of some or all of these things. This is the truth of real rather than literary depictions of suicide. And it's not the slightest bit glamorous. Björk would not be singing at the funeral of the depressed drunk who couldn't find a way through a mountain of bills, or at the funeral of the lonely teenage girl who is bullied at school. There may be no shame in suicide, as the Church once believed, but there is no glory in it either.

Albert Camus famously wrote: 'There is but one truly serious philosophical problem, and that is suicide.' I don't like this formulation and its cheap gravitas. It makes the whole life-or-death thing seem so appealingly dramatic – a drama in which you are always cast as the star. It turns you into some sort of Hamlet, being terribly profound with his 'to be or not to be' soliloquy, rather than into someone who needs to find help to tackle some of the more prosaic problems of life. If suicide is on your mind, beware all the self-obsessed drama of the existentialists, the poets and the fashionistas. Don't cast yourself as some romantic hero, living so intensely

7

because you are precariously perched on the narrow ledge between life and death. Make getting better into a form of work. Phone the Samaritans. Go and see your GP and take the pills you need to take. Talk to friends. Stop drinking. Misery is survivable. The problem is, when submerged in darkness, all this sounds too glib, dismissive even. People gave me this advice, but at the time it made little difference.

3.

I didn't really know the source of my misery. The events of the previous few months, with my resignation from St Paul's Cathedral and the subsequent deterioration of my marriage, were hard enough. But there was something else, something I couldn't decipher. And so, after that desperate sleepless night, I came up with a plan. It wasn't a bad plan, and it may have saved my life. But I didn't realize what it involved. That plan was to write it all down, to put on paper all the stuff that had brought me to this point. My initial thought was that I might be some sort of Scheherazade to myself, pushing back the darkness by telling my own story. I suppose one might call it an attempt at salvation through autobiography – which could be another way of describing what the Church has traditionally called confession. Or maybe it was nothing more than a delaying tactic, keeping myself mesmerized by language and well away from the rope shop. Indeed, had things turned out differently, there was every chance that this book could have ended up as a very long suicide note. But even as the dawn broke over my coffee-and-cigarette breakfast, I had some inkling that this was the right way to go.

I decided to put my faith in the healing power of words. I decided that self-narration, or re-narration, could be a

8

powerful way of putting the pieces back together. That it might just be a way to be reborn in the face of this horrendous feeling of emptiness, filling the hole with words that could provide the scaffolding for some new, brighter perspective. Isn't that what Freud promised? Using words to cure a sickness of the soul? And now it had got to this last desperate stage I might as well be honest. There was a certain giddy liberation in that thought. I had nothing left to lose. Anyway, nothing could be worse than this. Not even telling the truth.

4.

There were two major problems with the plan, not immediately apparent at the time. The first was what one might call the problem of truth. The second was what I will call the problem of salvation.

The problem of truth is familiar territory. I had promised myself that I would tell the truth, and that, as the saying goes, the truth would set me free. But one does not have to be Pontius Pilate to recognize that telling the truth, especially about oneself, is not a straightforward business. First, there is the problem of knowing what the truth is. And then there is the problem of telling it. It is worth going slowly and methodically here, for there are still a great many traps and opportunities for deception.

The problem of knowing the truth is not just a problem of self-knowledge, although it is that too. And much of what follows will be about the discovery of things – about myself and my ancestors – that I did not know before I started writing. But telling the truth about oneself is trickier than simply finding out stuff and then writing it down, because for one thing – unlike the more straightforward biography – when it comes to autobiography the person you are writing about changes in the very act of writing. Autobiography involves a moving target. Put simply, the writing of this book has changed me and thus changed the thing that I was writing about.

Of course, that was precisely the intention. It was undertaken as a writing cure, as narrative medicine. And (spoiler alert) it worked. Yes, there were lots of other unexpected interventions that helped me to get better – not least the decision to go into therapy. But the book was certainly a part of the healing process, and the process worked like this. I would write. I would live with what I had written and the way I had written it. I would apply critical pressure to the image of myself I was presenting, and then I would invariably delete what I had written, unsatisfied with the writing and the 'me' that I was discovering.

Early versions of this book revealed to me things about myself of which I was ashamed. Consider, for instance, the last few sentences of the previous section – 'I had nothing left to lose. Anyway, nothing could be worse than this. Not even telling the truth.' I first wrote those words in 2013. As I now write these words in 2017, a lot has changed. When I originally wrote those words, I was trying to soften up the reader to accept a version of my story in which I had been hard done by; in which I was the hero and others were the villains. The truth I had in my head in 2013 was the achieving of a sort of revenge – by means of a spiteful suicide note, dripping with anger and a narcissistic sense of injury. Back then, I wrote down names, dates and details in an explosion of resentment. Such was my apocalyptic mindset.

Thank God for the delete button. Thank God for my fabulously patient publishers, who allowed me the time to go through the lengthy process of healing. Had they pressed me for earlier versions of this manuscript, I would have set in ink a version of myself from which I might never have escaped.

This, then, is how I began to write. I told the blank screen who I thought I was and then I looked over what I had written and tried to live with it for a while. Even then, things I had written bothered me. It was not that I had chosen the wrong adjectives, or something like that. What concerned me was whether I was being honest or manipulative. Whether I had rightly understood myself, or was settling for the fake news coming from my ego. Whether in fact the person who was writing this book was someone I was proud of being.

In other words, the writing became a form of spiritual confession. I wrote things down, and the words would bring to life a person on the computer screen. I looked at this person and he looked back at me. I articulated the reality of who I thought I was and then I was judged by it, or shamed by it, or moved by it. This sort of writing can change a person. The subject of this autobiography began to feel continually slippery and elusive. There were times when I wondered how well I knew my subject.

There is another truth problem, of course. Autobiographies should never be wholly trusted. Any half-critical reader should rightly be suspicious of an autobiography that opens with an admission of suicidal intent. Unhappy people can frequently be highly manipulative. Furthermore, like everyone else, I wanted to tell you that I am better than I really am, that I am wittier, sexier and cleverer, that I am right when others are wrong. Even when I am being self-deprecatingly honest, I am surely being strategic for some advantage. Will any negative self-exposure contained in these pages be a sort of loss leader that makes credible the portrait of some higher nobility? So don't trust me. I don't even trust myself.

And finally, the truth – do you really think I am going to give you the whole truth? What makes you think you have the right to it anyway?

5.

The second problem is more complex and took a long time to come into view. The theologian in me wants to call it the problem of salvation; that is, the problem of how we come to heal from some fundamental human brokenness – and whether this healing requires the intervention of something or someone beyond the self. Are we able to sort ourselves out, unaided?

Interestingly, the very first of the famous twelve steps of the Alcoholics Anonymous programme is to 'admit that we are powerless over our addiction'. Before we embark on searching moral audits and the rest of it, the first move has to be an admission of thoroughgoing powerlessness. In other words, however else I am going to be saved from my troubles, salvation is not going to originate in me. I am not going to be the author of my own happiness.

But wasn't self-salvation precisely the plan? To bury deeper and deeper into my troubles, thus exposing them to myself and allowing the truth to set me free? Was my plan doomed from the start? Heidegger once said that 'only a god can save us now' – and what I think he meant was that the things that have the ability to save us, that dramatically change our situation, can only come from without – for instance, the love of another person or the love of God. That sort of thing cannot be cajoled or bullied into existence. The dawn from on high will just break on us. It comes at us, by surprise, from without. And we simply have to be patient and wait for it.

Prayer, wrote Rowan Williams, is a bit like sunbathing. Two things are necessary: first, you must take your clothes off; and second, you must lie in the light. In other words, you must be prepared for exposure – be honest with God and with yourself. And you must stay in that place where God – the light – can get at you. Preparation aside, it is not something you do, as much as something that is done to you. There is no hurrying this process along. It takes the times it takes.

So how can writing about the self possibly help? Isn't there an argument that it may only deepen the problem, pushing the self ever further into itself, into the deluded matrix of the me, me, me? From a theological perspective, what it requires is an altogether different direction, something that Christians used to call self-forgetfulness, for instance. When I was a university chaplain in Oxford, I used to advise self-absorbed students to stop talking endlessly about themselves and spend more time looking after those less fortunate. Spend some time, especially with those in real distress, and your own problems tend to miraculously disappear. Or, at least, they no longer seem so urgent. Not only is autobiography of no help in finding healing, it can actually be counter-productive.

But there is another way of looking at this problem, and this is inspired by the greatest theological genius of them all, Augustine of Hippo. Augustine's theology is built around the idea of waiting on God, on what Christians call grace. But Augustine also reinvented writing about the self. And the two concepts are intimately connected.

The literary form of the autobiography is commonly traced back to the apologia – a self-justifying response in the face of an accusation. Socrates was accused of atheism – or at least of dangerous theological innovation – and of corrupting the young. The way Plato covers the trial, the reader is led to imagine Socrates being fitted up by the mob. The apologia is a protestation of innocence in the face of an accusation of guilt. The spin-doctors who work to restore the tarnished reputations of public figures are familiar with many of its shadier rhetorical manoeuvres: from outright denial, to strategic omission, to blame-shifting, to the non-apology apology. Rightly, our suspicious age has become increasingly alert to these tactical evasions.

Suppose the accused does not plead his innocence but instead opens with an admission of guilt? Is suspicion thereby averted? After all, what does the openly guilty person need to defend himself against? This was St Augustine's technique in his *Confessions* and it transformed the whole genre of writing about the self. Indeed, the modern confessional autobiography, with all its overly emotional, public laundry-washing, is impossible to imagine without the development of Augustine's notion of original sin – that inescapable confession of human corruption. Furthermore, if God's judgement is the ultimate court of judgement, and our justification comes from Him alone and not from the approval of any human audience, then surely we can more easily tell the truth about ourselves to others without the fear of inconsequential human judgement. If one genuinely has only God to fear, and God knows all the secrets of our hearts, then what purpose is there in self-serving bullshit? In other words – so the argument goes – only something like Augustinian faith makes authentic autobiography possible. And this is where things get theologically and psychologically interesting – because, of course, there is much to be suspicious of here too. Before we come to that, let me allow the Augustinian argument to run a little longer – as Augustine is the hero of this book. He was a man of such exceptional self-knowledge and self-critical vigilance that I find myself returning to his light time and again. As I understand it, Augustine's much-misunderstood notion of original sin is not so much that human beings are shot through with sexual depravity – though sex is always a significant part of the story – nor that we are miserable sinners in any self-flagellating, life-denying sort of way, but rather that human beings are fundamentally broken. In other words, sin is not some secret shame but a feature of our common humanity. Original sin is badly named: it really should be called unoriginal sin because it is a part of all of us, and is mostly configured in the same way. Sin is original only in terms of its origination. Properly understood, sin is Christian language for human nature.

This existential brokenness is, crucially, not something we are able to put right on our own. We are not self-justifying creatures as Augustine's ideological arch enemy Pelagius maintained, but often, and frequently, despite our best efforts, at the mercy of powerful currents of irrationality and wilful self-destructiveness – even as children. This is why the self-serving apologia of the person intent on defending their ultimate innocence is little better than a nest of lies and of no help in finding salvation. But if the Christian world view is correct, then the saving grace – and I say that deliberately – is that the centre of gravity of human life is located outside our own individual selves.

This is the terrifying risk of Augustinian Christianity: we are reliant on something outside ourselves in order to be made well, complete and more fully human. To use a Reformation formulation, we are justified by divine grace and not by our own efforts or noble deeds. This means we can drop the apologetics and the need for any sort of defensive self-protectiveness. It doesn't matter what anybody else thinks of me. Ultimately, it doesn't even matter what I think of me. So I can stop pretending. Imagine how someone would write if they genuinely didn't give a damn what the reader thought of them. That's the theory, at least – Augustinian faith makes something like honest autobiography possible.

6.

Augustine's position makes more sense when contrasted with those of his theological opponents, most notably with that of Pelagius. Pelagius, so his detractors sneered, was a fat northern layman 'full of porridge'. Unfortunately, unlike Augustine, Pelagius does not come to us via his own words, but at second hand and filtered through the hostility of his opponents. It matters not whether they were being fair about him (it's safe to assume they were not): the battle between Augustine and Pelagius was one of ideas, not reputations, a battle over the essential nature of Christianity, indeed, over the very possibility of human virtue.

Pelagius was appalled at Augustine's position, which he believed to be an alibi for moral laxity. As the debate grew fiercer, the Pelagians used Augustine's openness about his mother's drinking habits and the pleasure he took in stealing fruit as a child as propaganda against him. But the particular phrase that really set Pelagius off concerned Augustine's apparent nonchalance regarding sexual morality: 'You command continence,' Augustine had written. 'Grant what you command, and command what you please.' In other words, if God wants me to be sexually chaste, it's down to Him to show me how to do it. It was a more philosophically sophisticated version of Augustine's witty teenage prayer: 'God grant me chastity and continence – but not yet.' Augustine,

Pelagius thought, was passing the buck and evading personal responsibility.

In this regard, Pelagius is much closer to modern sensibilities. Despite the fact that he was very much a distant theologian of the late Roman Empire, and despite his zealous asceticism, his commitment to individual freedom and personal responsibility, his sense that we are all innocent until proven guilty (babies thus being innocent), his confidence that the law is able to track the fullness of our moral concerns and his passionate belief in the intrinsic goodness of human beings chimes neatly with the contemporary Western mindset. Indeed, one might even say this applies specifically to the secular liberal mindset, for, as one of his most effective proponents, Bishop Julian of Eclanum, later argued, our moral autonomy is such that human beings are effectively 'emancipated from God'. When it comes to questions of right and wrong, and of our ultimate success or failure in the whole human enterprise, it's all down to us as individuals. This was much nearer to Stoicism than it was to authentic Christianity, Augustine insisted.

Pelagius' message was simple and powerful: be good and you will go to heaven. For him, being good meant nothing more (and nothing less) than abiding by all the rules and God's moral laws. The rules were those laid down in the Scriptures. 'Be perfect as your heavenly father is perfect' was his big sermon idea. His argument was that if God has told us to obey the rules, then it must be possible to obey the rules because God wouldn't ask us to do the impossible. And if it is possible, then it is obligatory. Like all easily communicated messages, it has a strong top line: be good and you will enjoy eternal reward. Perhaps it is the strength and simplicity of the message that explains how this position came to be so readily confused with orthodox Christianity, despite the fact that it was repeatedly condemned as the very epitome of heresy, first by the Council of Carthage in 418 and by the official Church ever since. And, in terms of the history of ideas, it is with this condemnation that the ancient world gives way to the Middle Ages.

What niggled Augustine about Pelagius' position was the unproblematic confidence with which he believed human goodness to be just a matter of getting on with it in a no-nonsense sort of way. Augustine's messy life had taught him that human beings are riddled with a complex set of motivations; that goodness is something we often want as an aspiration, but something we rarely achieve without qualification. Thus, if God requires human beings to be perfect as a condition of eternal reward, then, in reality, he is damning the entire human race to hell. This was something that Martin Luther was to wrestle with centuries later, concluding that if God required the unqualified goodness of human beings in order for them to be saved, then God was a total bastard and Luther hated Him. Later still, in 1931, Sigmund Freud made a secularized version of the same point when he wrote to Arnold Zweig: 'To be a biographer you must tie yourself up in lies, concealments, hypocrisies, false colourings and even in hiding a lack of understanding . . . And anyway, isn't our Prince Hamlet right, if we all had our deserts, which of us wouldn't escape whipping?'

The concept of original sin is often condemned as harsh and judgemental – as if to speak of human beings as ontologically sinful is somehow to rubbish them and denigrate the beauty of human life. Talk of sin instinctively feels repressive. In fact, the reverse is true. For if our wills are corrupted by Adam's fall and human beings are congenitally incapable of moral perfection – the message of original sin – then it is a profound cruelty to require perfection of us. We are being set up to fail. If the idea of original sin is to be criticized, it is surely from the opposite direction: that it is unduly permissive, that it provides weakness and immorality with a perfect excuse; and that it places human life beyond good and evil.

Augustine had another problem with Pelagius' position: it didn't give God any real work to do. If we gain entry to heaven by ticking all the moral boxes, then God's role in human salvation is that of a glorified compliance officer. And if the boxes have been ticked, then He has no discretion in granting to the virtuous entry to heaven or refusing it to the sinful. Effectively, salvation has been automated. Augustine argued this detracted from God's omnipotence and discretion – surely He could do what He wanted. After all, heaven was His creation and He could allow in whomever He pleased.

For Augustine, salvation is top-down, not bottom-up – like sunbathing. We are saved, he insists, not through any work of our own, not because of any virtue we may have acquired, including through our own meagre efforts, but entirely through grace, and gratuitously. That is, at God's own discretion and on His initiative. The problem with Pelagius is that he wanted to be his own redeemer, whereas for Augustine we don't have much of a hand in it. We can make our confession, publish our autobiography in all its moral ambiguity, and the rest is down to God. Publish and be damned – or saved. Let the chips fall where they will.

Pelagius was outraged. Augustine was granting human beings licence to behave as they wished. They could be the biggest shits of all time and yet God could end up forgiving them and granting them salvation. Could God redeem Stalin or Pol Pot? If so, what then of fairness? What of justice?

Thus far I have used terms like 'God' and 'heaven' as if they were entirely unproblematic. They were unproblematic for both Augustine and Pelagius, but they are certainly not for me. To state the obvious: the so-called masters of suspicion – that unholy trinity of Nietzsche, Marx and Freud, to say nothing of the Enlightenment – have problematized religious belief in a way that would have been unimaginable to anyone living in the fifth century.

It is worth contemplating how structurally similar Augustine's position is to that of Freud, whose atheistic credentials are impeccable. Indeed, I think of Augustine as having prefigured Freud in his central observation about human existence. Freud did not speak of 'original sin' but of 'original helplessness'. And, like Augustine, he insists that human beings are not in control of the sources of their own satisfaction – tellingly, a word that is central to both the psychoanalytic and theological enterprises.

For Freud, human beings are fundamentally vulnerable and dependent. Both Augustine and Freud were obsessed with babies – and for the same reason. The fury of the child is at not being able to satisfy its own cravings – for food, for comfort, for milk, for love. All the essential things in life – the very things without which life would not be possible – are provided for from beyond its control. The unattended baby will cry for help, for satisfaction. Without that, it will eventually die. And, like Augustine, for Freud the story of human life is substantially about how we adjust ourselves to this sense of not being in control. Indeed, we never quite recover from our childhood. It's another, albeit atheistic, version of anti-Pelagianism: we are not able to fix ourselves. We are not in charge of ourselves. We are helpless, powerless, impotent.

One familiar response to this 'original helplessness' is to pretend that it doesn't exist, that one can achieve some sort of existential self-sufficiency. In Christian terms, this can be rendered as the denial of our need for God, or at least the pretence that we can become mini-gods ourselves, that we can self-satisfy. But this fiction of human omnipotence can only be achieved by a disavowal of our own profound need for relationships, and this way madness lies. As the French analyst Serge Viderman put it, 'The hell of the narcissist is the tyranny of his need for others.' Applying all this to Pelagius, one might say that his insistence that human beings are capable of fully obeying moral rules, thus to guarantee for themselves ultimate satisfaction, was the thinking of a man terrified about his own lack of control, unable to countenance a life that was not finally subject to his own will. The ultimate Christian narcissist, he was a person incapable of being incapable.

Superficially, it looks as if Augustine is the narcissist. After all, he is the one who writes the autobiography. But narcissism is not the same thing as talking too much about yourself. Rather, the narcissist is the person who chooses self-reliance over reliance on other people (or, in Christian terms, on God). It is a refusal of the relational, a turning away from other people out of a fear that our need for love can never be met by others – and so it has to be self-generated.

What finally makes the narcissist's position some sort of silent nightmare is that the vulnerability from which the narcissist runs is not a wound or a weakness from which he or they need healing, but the very means by which human satisfaction is possible. For example, the child asks the father to play Lego with them. But Dad has to make an important call, and tells the child they can play in half an hour. 'OK, don't bother,' comes the child's response, cutting the father off. Unable to cope with their own need for others, and the frustrations that inevitably accompany such need, the child thereby sabotages their own happiness. This is the typical shape of narcissism, though obviously the trauma is often considerably more intense than that involved in this example. Narcissism, to use psychoanalyst Neville Symington's phrase, is a turning away from the life-giving other. Unable to cope with the possibility of rejection, Narcissus chooses the dead zone of non-relational safety and auto-satisfaction. In the end, he emotionally commits suicide.

The narcissist's hell is the ultimate locked-in syndrome because vulnerability is the way we are porous to others and they are porous to us; in other words, vulnerability is the way we are open to love. As my friend the psychotherapist Adam Phillips puts it: 'No helplessness, no satisfaction. Helplessness – which is so difficult to find a picture of for the adult that is not simply terrifying – is the precondition of satisfaction. If we lose, or forget, or repress, or project, or attack this original helplessness, we quite literally lose, in Freud's terms, the real possibilities of satisfaction. . . . Helplessness, Freud is suggesting, is the most important thing about us.' Augustine would agree, wholeheartedly. In Christian terms, the wound we are bequeathed as children of Adam, the wound of original sin, is not so much a wound as a gift: it is the very means by which we recognize our dependency on God and thus the very means through which He comes to us as our saviour.

Furthermore, it is only through an acknowledgement of our dependency that we can begin to develop a moral imagination that is not in hock to some unrealistic ideal of human perfectibility. As Freud puts it, 'the original helplessness of all human beings is thus the primal source of all moral motives'. If we are dependent on others, then they are dependent on us. Which means that all human beings come stamped with the request: 'Fragile – handle with care.' It is in response to this request that we instinctively care for human infants. As adults, nowhere is this combination of fragility and dependency more fully realized than when it comes to sex. If Freud and Augustine are sex-obsessed, it is precisely because sex represents a heightened form of vulnerability and thus holds out the possibility of heightened satisfaction. Indeed, isn't it remarkable that the word 'satisfaction' fits so appropriately into a sentence about sex as well as a sentence about God?

Masturbation, of course, is satisfaction without vulnerability. It is, as it were, Pelagian sex – the illusion of omnipotence as achieved via the refusal of risk. I am obviously being deliberately rude about Pelagius here: it is more than likely that he was a strict celibate. But masturbation and celibacy can share a common pathology: both can cooperate with the illusion of our own omnipotence by making the world as small as possible; ultimately, a world of one. Yet even masturbation cannot fully escape the presence of the other. For it is never simply a mechanical action, but also an act of the imagination. And the imagination taunts the pretence of masturbatory omnipotence by conjuring images of other people. Yet when we reach out to touch real people, reaching out beyond the locked-in syndrome of auto-satisfaction, we encounter the possibility of rejection that has the potential to unravel the very core of our being. Other people are not the puppets of our imagination or desire. Being chosen or not being chosen, that is where heaven and hell divide.

Here, then, is the issue at hand. Augustine's position is that a brave acknowledgement of human vulnerability is not only the precondition of honest self-exposure, but also the very condition of human flourishing. We can only tell the truth about ourselves when we appreciate that it's not all about us; that we are dependent on forces partially beyond our control. Wallace Stevens put it thus:

> From this the poem springs: that we live in a place
> That is not our own and, much more, not ourselves
> And hard it is in spite of blazoned days.

Hard it is, indeed.

The defensive approach is to hedge our vulnerability, not to invest in others, not to invest in that which is beyond our control. But this defensive position of divestment is ultimately self-defeating. Safe in our fortress, we wither away and die. Love that remains locked away exists in a permanent state of negative equity. On the other hand, if we risk venturing forth beyond our emotional defences, we are exposed to the possibility of rejection. For my money, Adam Phillips can sometimes feel just a little too nonchalant about the devastation that such rejection can bring. St Paul too, with his whole strength-in-weakness line. Vulnerability is terrifying because rejection can be catastrophic. 'We are desiring creatures and endangered by our desiring,' Phillips says. But he does so without a trace of panic in his voice.

2. Resignation

I.

On the afternoon of 26 October 2011, the Chapter of St Paul's Cathedral came together for a hastily convened meeting. We gathered in the Dean's private dining room with its long table covered in neat green baize, overlooking the communal gardens of Amen Court. Normally, we would meet over in the Chapter House, the official building for Chapter business, with a carefully prepared agenda. But this was different. An emergency situation. And it required privacy.

Tucked away between Wren's great cathedral and the Old Bailey, Amen Court consists of a collection of several impressive residences, some late seventeenth century, some Victorian, all designed for the canons of the cathedral Chapter. Throughout the year, various tourists on the London ghost tour would appear at the gate of the gloomy cul-de-sac, looking for the black dog of Newgate Prison – the vengeful reincarnation of an unfortunate inmate who had apparently been cannibalized by his fellow prisoners. But apart from the tourists, it was generally a pretty quiet place. Built around two small lawns with rose bushes and a collapsing damson tree, Amen Court was an oasis of ecclesiastical calm in the heart of the city. Here it was possible to forget that you were deep in the engine-room of global capitalism. In happier times, Chapter members would sit out on the grass and read, passing the time of day with a mixture of gentle church gossip and the occasional gin and tonic. But these were no longer the happiest of times. And today there was only one item on the agenda: the eviction of Occupy.

From the early Middle Ages, English cathedrals have jealously preserved their autonomy from the wider Church like mini city-states. It is often assumed that the Church functions with a clear command-and-control structure of authority, with the Pope or, following the Reformation, the Archbishop of Canterbury, having the ultimate say in all matters ecclesiastical. In reality, the Church is a complex web of checks and balances, with a strong emphasis on the independent authority of Church councils developing from the fourteenth century onwards. In the Catholic Church, this medieval drift towards greater subsidiarity was only decisively overturned at the First Vatican Council in 1869–70, where papal infallibility was finally established. But this controversial Roman Catholic innovation had little bearing on the Church of England, which is why many of the ancient cathedral Chapters remain the final source of authority for what happens in the cathedral – not the Bishop of London, not even the Archbishop of Canterbury. They retain a great deal of moral authority, of course, but executive authority rests with the Chapter. And so, in the matter of Occupy, the decisions were ours to make. And the higher-ups were mightily glad of it.

Because the meeting was called quickly, two of the eight members of Chapter were unable to attend, both of them so-called lay canons, non-clerical members with proper jobs elsewhere. One was at another meeting in the City, another was teaching in Oxford. They would cast their vote later, by email. But it probably didn't matter that they weren't present because we had all rehearsed our positions a number of times before and there were no surprises in what we said to each other. On the right of the argument, one of the canons was uncompromising: 'I'm not in water-canon mood,' he had declared, only half-joking, 'I'm in flame-thrower mood.' The Dean too, with a chairman's casting vote up his sleeve, was clearly fed up with the intrusion Occupy presented. The argument from this side was clear: Occupy had arrived uninvited. They were disrupting the worshipping life of the cathedral, causing chaos, losing us money and turning the Chapter, not to mention the wider Church, into a laughing stock. Enough was enough. Until it came to me, only my friend Mark Oakley, the Canon Treasurer, thought the matter was not so clear-cut.

The Chapter knew that I saw things differently. At this meeting, however, I found words impossible to come by – I was too emotional. And the more they pressed for eviction, the more I felt unable to speak. Their conclusion felt like a train coming at me in a tunnel. The mistake they were making seemed so blindingly obvious to me. So obvious that I just wanted to shout: 'Can't you see, can't you see?' – which isn't much of an argument. What was at stake was my whole understanding of the Gospel. Pretty much everything I believed about where the Church should stand on things was being unravelled. And there was nothing I could do to stop it. The mathematics seemed certain, even before I said a word. Those who supported eviction had four votes out of eight, plus the Dean's casting vote if necessary. It was a done deal. What was the point of more words?

It was the Dean who broke my silence. When it became obvious that I really had to say something, he reached across the baize table to hold my hand. We saw things from totally different points of view. He, too, was tired and angry, but he knew I needed encouragement in order to speak. It was a characteristic act of kindness. Some days earlier, the then Mayor of London, Boris Johnson, had phoned up the Dean to encourage him to sack me. The Dean told him that it was none of his business. I always felt enormously supported by the Dean.

And so it was that my final volleys against eviction – that we had turned Wren's building into an idol, a museum for the 1 per cent, that this was so much more than a little local difficulty, that the reputation of the Church was at stake – was launched with eviction's most powerful proponent squeezing my hand and urging me on to speak through watery eyes. It wasn't just his generous collegiality. I suspect I also spoke for a little part of him too. We were all conflicted, to a greater or lesser degree.

The decision went as expected. Though when the votes came in from the two absent lay Canons, it turned out that they had both voted against eviction. Chapter was evenly split, four in favour of eviction, four against. It was at half past nine in the evening when the Dean sent round a short email. He had used his casting vote, casting a second vote to break the deadlock. The motion was carried. Eviction it was to be.

An hour later I rang the Dean's doorbell and handed him the letter personally. I couldn't just pop it through his letterbox; I had to put it in his hand. He knew exactly what it was.

Dear Mr Dean,

These have been very difficult days for us all at the cathedral and I want to thank you a great deal for the generous way in which you have led us though this testing period. I feel hugely privileged to have been a part of the thoughtful discussions we have had since the protest camp arrived. And I also want to thank you personally for your sustained kindness towards me throughout my time at St Paul's. So it is without any sort of acrimony or bad feeling that I regret to say that I cannot travel down the path that Chapter has now chosen.

I have been clear and calm in my own mind that I will not be able to sign up to any course of action that may result in violence done in the name of the Church. And I feel that the decision we made this afternoon makes that a real possibility.

Obviously, my decision to leave has very significant consequences for me and my family – not least that I will have to find myself another job. I would very much appreciate a conversation with you about what period of notice you and Chapter would be comfortable allowing me.

With love,
Giles

2.

The protesters had first arrived on the afternoon of Saturday, 15 October, some streaming out of the tube station, others up Ludgate Hill. Perhaps 3,000 of them, no more. Certainly no more than St Paul's was regularly used to dealing with at many of its services. But these were different. They were mostly younger and came with banners and musical instruments. The sun was shining. The atmosphere was carnivalesque – more a festival than a demo. And it certainly wasn't the 'professional demonstrators' from central casting as they were later to be characterized. As the protest continued, many tried to pigeon-hole the Occupiers as public-school hypocrites or smelly long-haired layabouts. Later on, the camp would be pilloried for attracting the homeless and those with drug and alcohol abuse problems, as if such people had no place at so grand a palace as St Paul's. Occupy had multiple messages and it encompassed a huge diversity of people. Some wore anarchist masks, some brought picnic baskets.

What brought all these people together was a visceral sense of injustice about the way in which capitalism had developed – those it benefited and those it didn't. The backdrop was the financial collapse of 2007–2008 and the ways in which central government had responded to a crisis in banking – a crisis of the banks' own making – by bailing them out with public money. The cause of the financial crisis can itself be traced back to the deregulation of the City under Margaret Thatcher in 1986. The so-called Big Bang eventually transformed relatively sleepy financial institutions into high-class, high-stakes gambling dens. High-street banks became investment banks, borrowing vast amounts of money to play in the twenty-four-hours-a-day globalized casino of the increasingly complex financial markets. Indeed, so complex were the new financial instruments that came to be invented that most banks weren't entirely sure where their money was being invested. Bad loans, many of them mortgages sold to people who hadn't the money to pay for them, were repackaged, and repackaged again, and sold on as a financial gold mine. In this way, debts were reclassified as assets. And so, when house prices collapsed and these debts were exposed as worthless, the global financial system was itself revealed as one enormous Ponzi scheme. Not only that, the banks hadn't just gambled away their own money, they had also gambled away the money we the public had entrusted to them – our savings. Some believed that the banks' cash machines were hours away from being shut down.

What happened next was, arguably, even worse. Some banks, like Lehman Brothers, went to the wall. Others were bailed out with public money. Billions and billions of pounds – money that we had given in taxes to the government to fix our roads and pay for nurses, soldiers and teachers – was handed over to the very same bankers who had paid themselves silly money to gamble away our savings. Their profits were a private gain, their losses a public responsibility. It was socialism for the rich.

Had national governments allowed banks to go bust, many would have lost their savings. So the banks were described as 'too big to fail'. Had they gone down, they would have brought down millions of ordinary people with them. It was a form of blackmail: bail us out or the country gets it. National governments blinked and paid up. This was the point at which it became obvious to many that the financial markets had become more powerful than national governments. Little wonder people wanted to protest.

The original aim of the protesters had been to occupy the London Stock Exchange in the adjacent Paternoster Square, a quadrangle of shiny new buildings that had taken its name from the Lord's Prayer. Despite its ecclesiastical title, it was, like a great deal of the City, private land. Ironically, it was land that the Church itself had sold off the year of the Big Bang, on a 250-year lease. As the Occupiers arrived, an injunction was taken out by the new owners to seal it off. Metal gates were erected at all the various entrances to Paternoster Square. Police and private security guards made the place impenetrable.

So it was that the protesters came to position themselves on the steps of Wren's magnificent cathedral. It made a natural amphitheatre. St Paul's may not have been the original destination venue for Occupy, but it is hard to imagine they would have achieved as much attention had they placed themselves anywhere else. St Paul's was designed as a stage for large national events. And, for a few months, it was to be precisely that.

Those who set themselves up on the cathedral steps on that balmy Saturday evening had no idea how long they would end up being there. Many thought the police would move them along during the night. At one point during that first evening a few hundred protesters were kettled in front of the cathedral, squashed together by a police cordon. But the level of agitation never rose much above the irritable. As the night wore on, a few dozen of the more determined Occupiers sat themselves down under the front portico, refusing to budge. In response, a line of police took up position shoulder to shoulder all the way along the west front, halfway up the steps. The Occupiers huddled together, smoking fags, waiting for the morning. The police maintained their line. The positions were set.

This was the scene that greeted me on the Sunday morning as I arrived at the cathedral early, still clutching my morning coffee. Here was the problem. It was 7.20 a.m. In another forty minutes there was to be an 8 a.m. Eucharist in the cathedral. This would generally attract several dozen people. But given that the police had blocked the entrance, there was no way of getting people into church. I was the Canon-in-Residence, basically the duty canon for the month and responsible for much of the day-to-day decision-making. Others would later question whether I had the authority to do what I did next, though it seemed perfectly obvious to me that I did. And anyway, there was no time for any sort of wider consultation. Worshippers would be arriving for the service in a few minutes.

I found out who was in operational command of the police – a sensible Sikh officer in a turban. I explained the problem and asked him if he would bring his officers down from the steps. I wasn't so concerned about all the other police around the rest of the cathedral. They had a job to do, I understood that. But I wagered that if the police came down from the steps, so too would the small band of huddled protesters. And so it turned out. As the police left, a group of Occupiers applauded and gathered round to ask me questions. 'Are we welcome to come to church?' Well, that one was a no-brainer. Everyone is welcome to church. 'Do you believe in the right of people peacefully to protest?' That was a no-brainer too. Of course I did. What I explicitly did not do was issue an invitation for the protesters to camp outside the cathedral. It wasn't about granting permission. Clearly, I had no authority to do that.

The newspapers, however, thought I was making a political statement. 'Move along, please, Canon tells police as anti-bank protesters camp out at St Paul's' was the *Guardian*'s headline. The *Telegraph* had it thus: 'When police took to the steps of St Paul's Cathedral yesterday to protect it from hundreds of demonstrators protesting against the global financial system they were met with an unusual response. The Canon Chancellor of the cathedral asked police to leave, and instead welcomed some of the protesters to the Sunday morning service.' My welcome of the protesters to church soon slipped in the imagination of the press into a welcome for the protest camp itself – a subject on which I had been careful not to express a view. From here it was a small step to cast me as some latter-day Wat Tyler instigating a type of Peasants' Revolt.

The media representation of the events of St Paul's had a significant influence on how things played out. As the headlines got sharper, so the pressure within the cathedral and among my colleagues built up. Some clearly thought that I had deliberately invited the attention and were irritated by the way my apparent sympathies with the protesters reflected on the rest of them. I was asked to keep quiet and stay away from microphones. My own line was that those who are overly afraid of media attention too often become its victims. Simply to say 'no comment' is to paint a target on your back. The idea that a complex and fast-changing situation can be managed with bland press releases carefully constructed by a committee, whose purpose is to insist that there is nothing of interest going on, was never going to work. Fear of the press often creates a highly defensive mindset that is wary of anything but bland generalizations.

There was little doubt in my mind that the arrival of Occupy at St Paul's called for a specifically theological response, and not a response concerned most of all with press management. The principal weakness in the way the cathedral Chapter responded to the situation was that it involved very little corporate reflection on the big theological questions that were being raised. If you count up the number of references in the Bible, the right use of money and economic justice is the number-one moral issue, yet at no point did the Chapter have a sustained theological conversation about the merits or otherwise of the Occupy case.

At one point I suggested that we ought to do some Bible study before we were advised how to react by our lawyers. This was met with one of the few overt outbursts of anger by one Canon who thought it was an attempt to manipulate others by playing the faith card. Of course, this sort of manipulation does indeed go on in churches all the time. But to avoid theology altogether out of fear that it might prove divisive was a huge mistake. It left us without a distinctive response; instead we issued banal assertions of general support for all through the unconvincing language of the so-called media experts. It made us look like central-casting Anglicans, lacking any sort of conviction. But the truth is we all had convictions. It is just that they often pointed in different directions. That, of course, is both the strength and the weakness of the Church of England.

But disagreements of principle aside, we all agreed that we

had to do something. There was a sense in the first week after the arrival of Occupy that we were being led by events and were not in control of them. It was this pressure that led to the mistaken decision to close the cathedral to visitors on the grounds of health and safety. The interesting thing about this decision was not the personalities involved but the wider structural forces that led to it. St Paul's is a huge enterprise. It employs hundreds of people and manages nearly a million worshippers a year and roughly the same number of visitors again. It has a small army of masons and electricians and visitor managers and administrators. For some of these, working at St Paul's is a part of their Christian vocation. For others, perhaps the majority, their work is not so much for a church as for an iconic public building. I remember the Dean preaching a powerful sermon to the effect that if God was not at the heart and purpose of the building, then we might as well hand the keys over to the National Trust. He was right. Even so, for a significant number of people, St Paul's Cathedral was a building first, the ceremonial events it staged second, and a place of worship a distant third. Inevitably, therefore, the response many had to Occupy grew out of a concern for the building itself. The fact that it was a place of worship, inspired by a homeless carpenter from the Galilee, who spoke of the first being last and the last first, was regarded as pretty much beside the point.

The Chapter itself never actually met to discuss whether to close the building on the grounds of health and safety. An external adviser had been invited to look around the camp and had offered on-the-spot verbal advice that the place was unsafe. This was a view that would not be shared by the fire brigade when they were later pushed to say what they thought. Suggestions were even made that the fire brigade was afraid of their own unions, who might have been sympathetic to the

Occupy cause. But this was baseless speculation. In truth, when the Chapter saw the actual contents of the health and safety report a few days later, a number of us were concerned that it did not justify the closure. The press thought the whole thing was a stitch-up – unfavourably comparing the decision to close the cathedral with the determined defiance exhibited throughout the Blitz to keep St Paul's open. Our poor beleaguered press officer said she had her first moment of genuine panic when she saw the emails between Chapter members expressing incredulity at the contents of the report. It was her job to hold the line, but it was a line that was not convincing anyone.

While the cathedral was closed to the public the clergy met as usual for morning and evening prayer. With no congregation, it was an eerie and tense experience. We tried to do 'business as usual', though it was far from that. In that vast empty space, we dressed up in our cassocks, read the readings and said our prayers. Often the readings were just a little bit too directly and uncomfortably pertinent to our situation.

For some, the purpose of a cathedral is simply for the worship of God – and this was exactly what was being continued. It is a line of thought that is often used to explain why, even when so few people attend choral evensong, it is still worth having, paying for and training one of the greatest choirs in the world. Their singing is not directed to those sitting in the pew, but to God on behalf of us all. In this view, therefore, a cathedral of empty seats is almost a cathedral expressing itself in its purest form: divine worship, not a God-themed concert for culture-hungry tourists. For others, however, myself included, Christian worship had implications of openness and public proclamation which meant that prayers in a locked cathedral felt hollow and lacking in context. As we sat in the stillness, the Occupiers were making loads of noise outside. For some this was an intrusion. For others it was the world shouting to be let in – a view underlined by the fact that we met for our prayers beneath Holman Hunt's famous painting of Christ knocking on the door, demanding entry.

However, it was not the Occupiers but the City of London Corporation that were knocking the loudest. From the start, they were overwhelmingly hostile to the presence of the Occupy camp. Had they believed that they alone had a legal right to evict, they would certainly have done so straight away. But their problem was the legal ownership of the land on which Occupy had camped. For the extraordinary truth was that no one actually knew who owned the land – the cathedral or the Corporation. The lawyers were working furiously to sort that one out. But pressure from the Corporation meant that the Chapter was pressed to make a quick decision to join them in going down the legal route towards eviction. We were told we had twenty-four hours to decide. And we were advised by lawyers that on no account were we to negotiate with the protesters. To negotiate would imply that Occupy could be legitimately negotiated with, which would have given them de facto rights to stay and could create a permanent Parliament Square-type situation. Thus we were forced into making a decision: to evict or not to evict.

All my colleagues knew this was a red-line issue for me. The protesters were peaceful. They were not interfering with anyone's rights of access to the cathedral and they were raising an issue of profound public concern about the nature of ethical capitalism – a concern that it had been my job on the Chapter to encourage debate on. Furthermore, it was obvious that, especially in those early days, and given the large numbers of protesters camping outside the cathedral, eviction contained a very serious risk of violence – violence done in the name of the Church. I would not countenance putting my name to such a course of action.

The resignation itself was the easy bit. I had warned my family that it might come to this and explained things to my children by showing them a YouTube clip of the police clearing the Occupy Melbourne site, which was an especially ugly affair. They completely got it. The morning after I handed my letter of resignation to the Dean, I put it out on Twitter, and then went out for a coffee and a fag. It was at that point that things went bonkers.

When I returned to the house, a camera crew had already stationed itself outside Amen Court. I hadn't shaved that morning and was wearing a grubby black T-shirt and jeans. Had I been caught on camera looking like that, the Wat Tyler narrative would have been all the more convincing. So I fled over the Millennium Bridge to the Members' Room of the Tate Gallery. From up on the balcony there is a spectacular view of St Paul's. My phone kept ringing and ringing. My inbox was full of messages from the press. I wasn't going to answer anything. I sat quietly for an hour, heart pumping, mind doing somersaults.

But there was no hiding. I knew I had to try and take control of the situation or the story would end up being told by other people, without the facts. So I called Alan Rusbridger, a friend of mine and the editor of the *Guardian*. He told me to come over straight away and I got a cab up to King's Cross. The interview was comedy gold. We talked through all the usual stuff about politics and the Church. I tried to explain that it wasn't a them-and-us situation and that I was far less radical than people had presumed – that this wasn't about left or right, it was about faith. He wanted a photograph, but I was still scruffy and unshaven. Rusbridger remembers it thus:

He reluctantly agrees to be photographed. He borrows an electric razor and a white shirt, roaring with laughter as he strips to the waist in the editor's office. He pulls on his jacket. And, for the first time today, the Revd Dr Giles Fraser begins to look a little less like a protester and a touch more like the Canon of England's most majestic cathedral. Albeit an unemployed one.

The photographer did what they often want to do with the clergy and got a picture of me looking heavenwards with the carefully constructed lighting creating a halo effect on the wall behind. He took dozens of pictures. 'Look up,' he said at one point. I did. And so he got the shot he wanted for the front page of the next day's paper. I was falling into another clichéd narrative. Later, I would do an interview with Ruth Gledhill from *The Times*, still in Rusbridger's shirt. As I wandered over to meet her, I suddenly worried that they might make something of the soft drink that I had in my hand and its well-known advertising jingo: 'Dr Pepper, so misunderstood'. I was getting paranoid.

The prize for the most hostile commentary on my resignation had to go to Martin Samuel, a sports columnist, writing in the *Daily Mail*. His take was that the cathedral was really just a business and that my so-called 'welcome' to protesters was coming back to bite me. 'Giles Fraser, Canon Chancellor of St Paul's Cathedral, knows all about capitalism now. It isn't about slogans and protests and impassioned editorials in Left-leaning publications. It is about really mundane stuff, like passing trade and customer access and the bottom line. Things a clergyman wouldn't know a whole lot about.' He went on to sneer at the cost of a set lunch in the St Paul's restaurant, £25.95, and the expensive cufflinks sold in the shop. He thus managed to cast the cathedral as money-grubbing and financially naive at the same time. We couldn't win.

Others understood the whole thing from a completely different perspective. 'The protesters outside St Paul's are demanding an end to the reign of naked greed over our lives. It is a proposal in which one would expect Christians of conviction to play an active part. By turning them away, St Paul's has indicated that, whatever the church's spiritual message, for those who run the place its fabric is more important. That's a bureaucratic way of saying, yes, God is dead,' wrote Peter Popham in the *Independent*. That one I agreed with. Every national newspaper ran an editorial. Everyone had a view. Everyone had different advice. The storm blew in from all directions. In 2015 the Donmar Warehouse even put on a play about it, with Simon Russell Beale playing the Dean.

Soon I received a message that the Archbishop of Canterbury, Rowan Williams, wanted to see me. He had been away in Zimbabwe meeting Robert Mugabe. The Lambeth press office later joked that the success of that visit was soon eclipsed by the developing St Paul's story. I had known the Archbishop since I was a student of his at Oxford. He and I had had our differences over the gay issue, but we continued to have a warm relationship. He sent me a supportive email on hearing of my resignation.

Dear Giles,

This is just to say that I imagine this must be a pretty taxing time for you, and I wanted to send a word of support and prayer. You made a difficult and brave decision, and I honour you for that. Where it all goes now is anyone's guess, and plenty of people are exhibiting that distinctive brand of cost-free wisdom that characterizes the British media. I hope you're bearing up, anyway. You're prayed for here.

Love Rowan

Rowan sat me down in his study at Lambeth Palace and got me to explain what had been going on. He said I had done the right thing. We talked briefly about other jobs. I told him I had been approached about being the next Bishop of Edinburgh. He didn't seem to like that idea. He wanted me to stay in the Church of England. We spoke about the Deanery of Liverpool or of returning to be an inner-city parish priest. As I shook his hand to leave, we had a little chat about the American philosopher Stanley Cavell, in whose work we both had an interest. It was all very senior common room.

Something seemed to change on my lonely walk back from Lambeth Palace along the river to St Paul's. I suspect that a call might have been made at the Palace after I'd left, but I have no evidence to back this up. By the time I got home the then Bishop of London, Richard Chartres, wanted to see me. We had been together at the last service in St Paul's before the health and safety closure, and he also had written me a very generous note after my resignation. Again, he was kind and personally supportive. He asked me if I would be part of a task force – he called it the London Connection – led by the banker Ken Costa, the aim of which was to address some of the issues that had been raised by Occupy. He also asked me whether I would accompany him to the camp, show him around and introduce him to the protesters. This in itself was a significant development given the ridiculous legal advice that we had received, effectively banning us from speaking to the Occupiers.

At my induction at St Paul's one of my former parishioners had described the Bishop of London as the sort of bishop you would get at Harrods. That's about right. But Chartres was also very much at ease with ordinary people. He sat in the camp and chatted freely with the protesters. By this stage in the occupation, the camp itself was developing something of a complex infrastructure. There was the grandly named

Tent City University, a marquee where people drifted in and out to listen to many distinguished academics – economists, ecologists and theologians – who would come and try to make themselves heard over the noise of the traffic and the bells of the cathedral. Finding loos was a constant struggle, with the local Starbucks regularly used for changing and ablutions. People with masks and banners and instruments would come and go, most of them in their twenties. At the pop-up café, they made the Bishop a cup of tea. A keen environmentalist himself, he took a particular interest in their recycling processes. He joked and chatted about the bins. He was a class act. Maybe things were changing.

But the next day, a Sunday morning, it was an altogether different experience. The Bishop had persuaded the Dean that he also should go out and engage with the Occupiers. They would do it together. This was to be an unhappy affair, with the Dean looking tired and uncomfortable in front of the cameras. He later said that it was during the following service that he decided he also had to resign. As he said in a subsequent statement, 'I do this with great sadness, but I no longer believe that I am the right person to lead the Chapter of this great cathedral.' This was sad news indeed. He brought us all together at his house that evening and dropped the bombshell. It was the lowest moment of the whole affair. I left the room to give him a hug. I didn't know what to say. The next day the main headline in the *Telegraph* read: 'St Paul's branded a national joke.' It was a quote they had picked up from the local Tory MP, Mark Field, who apparently decided that this was a good opportunity to put the boot in. It was a thoroughly shitty thing to do.

With the Dean gone, the natural choice of acting Dean would have been the Canon-in-Residence. The Canon-in-Residence always chairs Chapter meetings when the Dean cannot attend, and chairing Chapter meetings is the principal job of the Dean as set out in his remarkably brief job description. The problem was that I was still the Canon-in-Residence – this was the last day of October and the end of my monthly stint. And there were a great number of people who were furious with me for apparently siding with the Occupiers. Though I had resigned, I had given the cathedral six months' notice. I was obliged by my contract to give at least three, but entitled to give six. Given the glacial pace of the Church of England recruitment process, I needed this length of time to find another job and find new schools for my children. But, as my colleagues pointed out, had I remained active in the cathedral, many would have felt this to be, in some way, an insult to the Dean. At a meeting the next morning, I was asked by my colleagues if I would take gardening leave and have nothing more to do with the cathedral. I agreed. I walked out of the meeting and that was it. I was never to have anything more to do with St Paul's – though I would continue to live in my house in the cathedral precincts for the next six months, which turned out to be the most stressful part of the whole affair.

The last service I attended in the cathedral was the Sunday evensong, at which I was listed to preach. The situation was incredibly tense, and a public sermon, with the press inevitably present, could easily have made matters worse. In such circumstances, there is a familiar ploy, often used by the clergy in difficult situations: you preach on the readings. The readings for any given service are set in advance on a three-year cycle. The sermon is meant to be an exposition of the texts set for that particular occasion. So, to be gently advised to 'preach on the readings' is also Anglican code for keeping your head down. The problem was that the person who suggested I preach on the readings hadn't actually looked at the readings. The Gospel text, it turned out, was from St Luke, chapter 6:

> As he lifted up his eyes on his disciples, and said, Blessed be ye poor: for yours is the kingdom of God. . . But woe unto you that are rich! For ye have received your consolation.

It was almost absurdly apposite and, given the circumstances, there was absolutely no way such a passage could be ignored. To do so would have been a betrayal of all belief and conviction. Indeed, the ferocity of a passage such as this stood in telling contrast to the hand-wringing approach of the cathedral spin doctors. Had a priest stood on the steps of St Paul's and uttered these words to the press during Occupy, he or she would have been accused of fermenting class warfare. The same could be said for the words of the Magnificat, again from St Luke (chapter 1), sung immediately before the Gospel reading.

> He hath put down the mighty from their seat: and hath
>   exulted the humble and meek.
> He hath filled the hungry with good things: and the rich
>   he hath sent empty away.

This passage is sung by the choir in the cathedral pretty much most evenings. As it is sung so beautifully – that evening it was to George Dyson's arrangement in F – it is easy to overlook that it feels a lot like a call to revolution. It is an intrinsic problem of cathedral worship: sometimes the whole experience can be so aesthetically impressive and agreeable that content loses out to the form. And, too easily, the form becomes an end in itself. When this happens, a cathedral can feel like a bejewelled dressing-up box that has lost touch with the extraordinary idea that, in the Christian tradition, God was born as a refugee in a cheap shed around the back of a pub. Even so, these Gospel passages are not straightforward, and it would have been utterly simplistic to read off from their contrast between the rich and the poor a version of that contrast being proclaimed on Occupy banners between the rich 1 per cent and the other 99 per cent. In truth, most of us there were rich.

As I climbed into that huge pulpit at St Paul's, my heart was in my mouth. I am dyslexic, so I often stumble when I have to read from a script. Early on in my time as a priest I learnt to preach without notes, which has the advantage of conveying immediacy, but also means that you don't always put things as carefully as you might had you written it all down beforehand. Would the pressure of this final sermon under the great dome at St Paul's mean that I would fluff my lines, or say something stupid, something I would come to regret? The situation felt extremely tense.

What I really wanted to do in the sermon was to challenge the perpetual temptation we all have to construct a narrative around what we do in which we are permanently the good guys. The Occupy protest was such an important release of frustration and indignation against an economic system that remained far too indifferent to its many casualties. Yet, as with so much political protest, there was a danger of a sense of self-righteousness about it, and – at worst – it could have had a nasty persecutory energy that demonized opponents. I suppose I wanted to draw upon any credit I might have acquired with a number of the protestors to challenge some of the uglier aspects of the Occupy movement.

The core of the sermon was borrowed from an essay by the great Jewish philosopher and sociologist Gillian Rose. Rose died of cancer in 1995, after a deathbed conversion to Anglicanism. A few years before, she had become a consultant to the Polish Commission for the Future of Auschwitz, helping them to think through how people experience the horror of the death camps as they pass through them. Rose argued that what was most potentially transformative about the whole experience was not simply the encouragement to identify with the victims, but also to develop some disturbing understanding of how the perpetrators did what they did, and how, in similar circumstances, one might even have been led to do the same. She wanted this experience to precipitate a kind of crisis in which the visitor would ask themselves if – just perhaps – they too would have been sucked in by such wickedness. This experience, she believed, would be far more morally transformative. 'Instead of emerging with sentimental tears, which leave us emotionally and politically intact,' Rose said, 'we [ought to] emerge with the dry eyes of a deep grief, which belongs to the recognition of our ineluctable grounding in the norms of the emotional and political culture represented.'

The message of Rose's essay had a massive impact on me. After reading it, I tried always to be alert to those forms of engagement that feel morally or politically powerful, but which 'leave us emotionally and politically intact' as if nothing life-changing had been learnt. The more transformative stuff, Rose was claiming, happens when we understand our own potential for, and complicity within, the things that we protest against. On the other hand, when we are simply and uncomplicatedly in the right – and all we have to do is shout about it – something in our moral imagination is diminished. I suspected that this was a danger with Occupy. There is sometimes an easy piety in protest that can make people close down their self-critical vigilance, and I wanted to challenge that, both in myself and in others. 'We all own shares in the way of the world,' I said. And we were all up to our necks in this economic system – mostly all beneficiaries, mostly all complicit.

At some point, as I was developing this theme, I made reference to my resignation. Someone in the congregation enthusiastically heckled their support and a murmur of support echoed under the dome. I suppose I should have been grateful. But this person had completely misunderstood what I had been saying. I don't think I have ever been so angry in the pulpit. With my Chapter colleagues in their seats behind me, this wasn't about some simple right versus wrong, and the Church wasn't some Punch and Judy show. Someone in the congregation that evening later wrote about it on Facebook.

When he mentioned his decision to resign, someone in the congregation shouted out, 'Congratulations!' I think if he'd given us one second we'd all have been on our feet with a standing ovation. Instead he came back instantly with a very firm, 'No. Absolutely not.' I could feel everyone around me reeling.

I half remember saying all of this. But after that heckle, it all came tumbling out in something of an emotional red mist. Reducing the issues at stake here into some cheap boo-hurrah was exactly what I didn't want to happen.

I've never heard a voice from the pulpit sound the way his did at the last sentence of his sermon. It wasn't a preacher voice at all, it was absolutely human, raw, and angry and left the congregation shocked. The last thing he said was: 'It's not supposed to be EASY!'

And it wasn't easy. The next morning, I went back into the vestry to collect my cassock. That was the last time I was to be in the cathedral as one of its canons.

For the next six months I would feel like *persona non grata* among my colleagues – though there was much support for me in public. Priests who I had been friendly with for years would cut me dead and refuse to speak with me. During the whole of that cold winter, the cathedral works department was mysteriously unable to come round to fix our heating at home, which had broken down. After three months, I received a letter from the Church of England Pensions Board thanking me for my service in the Church and letting me know my salary would be stopped at the end of the month. The cathedral had told the central Church body responsible for my salary that I had given them only three months' notice, which was not true. It was a pretty bleak time.

One of the most difficult things was how all this affected my faith. Cut off from the regular pattern of worship that had been central to my life at the cathedral, it was easy to drift. No longer was I part of a worshipping community which is so essential to the life of faith. No longer did I have an opportunity to celebrate the Eucharist, which is so essential to the life of a priest. My friends and family were worried about me. Indeed, I was worried about myself.

I did think about leaving the Church. In February, Alan Rusbridger offered me some work as a leader writer at the *Guardian* and I started to fill my days by going into the office at King's Cross every day. I thought it was the beginning of a mental and emotional rehabilitation. I said I would write about anything they liked as long as it wasn't about religion (though that didn't last long). Others suggested that I might be better going into politics. I went out to dinner with a couple of MPs in the House of Commons to discuss the matter. But it wasn't really my thing. During this time I realized that I am a priest to my boots. And besides, I don't think my views about politics make sense to many people. The one thing Occupy had demonstrated to me was that mainstream political life had become so safe and management-focused that it was no longer possible to say the things that many people wanted to say.

No, my future was in the Church. But where? And how? The Occupy movement had exposed a side to the Church that I found difficult to live with. But also, and much more mysteriously, it had begun to expose aspects of myself that I found difficult to cope with. St Paul's had been just a little bit too good for the ego, a little too satisfying. As a Canon, I was entitled to wear red buttons and trim on my cassock. One afternoon during my time at St Paul's, Archbishop Rowan Williams came into the vestry and teased me about them. 'Red buttons, Giles,' he smiled, 'it always begins with red buttons.' I knew what he meant. Ambition, pride, clericalism, self-satisfaction – they all started with red buttons.

The symbolic significance of the red buttons stayed with me long after that conversation. A few weeks after my resignation, I was contacted by a young portrait painter, Rebecca Cartwright de Fontenelle. Rebecca had just won a prize from the Royal Society of Portrait Painters to paint a subject of her choice. She asked if I would sit for her. I thought it would take just a few days, but Rebecca worked meticulously from life, never from photographs. Days turned into weeks. As she painted in my study at St Paul's, I stared out of the window and contemplated an uncertain future. My cassock hung behind the door. In the final portrait, the red buttons appear to come out of my ear. It couldn't have been more appropriate.

Rebecca has written that 'portraiture . . . makes a claim of knowing another person in a way which I believe is impossible'. Perhaps that is why I absolutely hated having my portrait painted. Rebecca was studying me closely, and I really didn't like it. It was as if she was searching for something that would in some way capture me. But I felt like there was nothing there to capture. The more she looked for it in my face, the more I felt the absence of whatever it was that I was missing. Her painting of me captures that slightly terrified vacancy rather brilliantly. My mother still cannot look at that portrait without crying.

The strange thing was that, within weeks of Rebecca's painting being finished, it would be a chance encounter with another portrait that would give me some sort of first clue as to what might be missing. This other painting was of similar size, painted nearly a century before. Unlike my portrait, the man who looked out from it had an untroubled gaze. It was a portrait of my ghost.

3. Ghosts

I.

Ghosts are psychological unfinished business. Like dreams, they constitute what Freud famously called a 'return of the repressed'. Ghosts are lost experiences looking for a home.

In *Beyond the Pleasure Principle*, Freud speculates that some traumatic experiences – such as those of war veterans – though initially suppressed by the desire to avoid mental pain (the pleasure principle), can sometimes reassert themselves in unexpected ways, in dreams or in various forms of self-destructive behaviour. What he calls the 'repetition compulsion' can occasionally override the pleasure principle so that the suppressed pain bubbles up into conscious experience. And this drama of repression and repetition doesn't just play out within the boundaries of the solitary individual, but as the Hungarian psychoanalysts Nicolas Abraham and Maria Torok emphasize, repressed traumas are able to spill over beyond the individual and can be passed down the generations. They call it 'transgenerational haunting'. This passed-on repression is often carried over in the form of family secrets. 'What haunts are not the dead, but the gaps left within us by the secrets of others.' It is the unsaid that spills repression over into future generations. It is the unsaid that bequeaths some curious flickering half-life to the undead. These are the traumas that have not received a proper burial. Too painful to mourn, they are avoided and handed down the family tree. This is where ghosts come from.

Towards the end of his life, suffering from throat cancer and having fled Vienna from the Nazis to find sanctuary in London, Freud also began to speculate about a curious form of transgenerational haunting. This was the basis of Freud's controversial, rather weird – and, to some, downright offensive – attempt to articulate the origins of Judaism in *Moses and Monotheism* (1939). His account goes like this. Moses wasn't Jewish. He was Egyptian. The baby hidden in the bulrushes narrative is just a cover story to disguise Moses' Egyptian origins. And indeed, the monotheism that Moses came to impose on the Jewish people was originally an Egyptian idea.

For Freud, this originally Egyptian but soon-to-be quintessentially Jewish idea, was the source of the peculiar genius of the Jewish people. Because God was not a thing or some being that could be experienced with the senses, because God was not an object like a golden calf, God could only be experienced internally. Thus, claims Freud, Moses invented the idea of an invisible God and with it the very capacity for abstract thought. 'The prohibition against making an image of God – the compulsion to worship a God whom one cannot see,' Freud argued, became a defining feature of the Jewish imagination: 'a sensory perception was given second place to what may be called an abstract idea – a triumph of intellectuality over sensuality'.

But so alien were the precepts of this strict new monotheism that the first Jews rebelled against it and murdered Moses in the desert. This, Freud maintained – on really no evidence whatsoever – was the founding trauma of Judaism. Generations later, the revival of this religion of Moses constituted a return of the repressed trauma. And through the force of repetition compulsion, Judaism was created and given transgenerational impetus. Because of the collective trauma associated with the murder of Moses, the religion of Moses was imprinted on the collective psyche of the Jews. The sins of the father were visited on the children and their children's children. Thus, for Freud, Judaism became a kind of collective ghost story.

And the point about ghosts is that they have a way of coming back to haunt us when we least expect them.

2.

It is January 2012 and I'm on the train to Liverpool, travelling north to an interview for a job that I do not want. Some weeks after my resignation from St Paul's I'd been to see Richard Chartres, the Bishop of London, and he suggested that I take a look at the Dean's job at Liverpool Cathedral. I wasn't enthusiastic. I'd had my fill of cathedrals over the previous few months and the prospect of running the largest cathedral in the country – indeed, the seventh largest in the world – filled me with dread. What I had come to conclude about the whole St Paul's/Occupy affair was that the building itself had been at the heart of the trouble. For too many of those involved, the preservation of those great stones of the cathedral had become the Church's primary purpose. Despite the fact that during every evensong the cathedral choir would tell the story of God bringing down the mighty from their seats and lifting up the lowly, when the lowly finally made an appearance outside the great West door of the cathedral the authorities at St Paul's chose to worship the architectural genius of Sir Christopher Wren instead. In the Hebrew Scriptures, they called it idolatry. St Paul's had become the golden calf. At least, that is how it all seemed to me. They chose temples over tents – which seemed more than a little ironic, given that St Paul was himself a tent-maker by profession.

But at least being the Dean of Liverpool's equally vast cathedral wouldn't come with anything like the same historical baggage as it did at St Paul's. However, I still had a suspicion that the job was mostly about real estate. Someone had told me that the mortar between the bricks was beginning to crumble. I really didn't want to be a glorified buildings manager. Nonetheless, I was going to have to give the interview my best shot. In terms of the greasy pole, it was a sensible enough thing to go for. Indeed, in less than a year the outgoing Dean of Liverpool, Justin Welby, was to end up as the new Archbishop of Canterbury. Still, this wasn't about ambition. I was going up to Liverpool because I didn't have much choice. There wasn't a plan B. In fact, there wasn't much of a plan A. I just needed a job. It turns out that tents are not as secure as temples.

But the emptiness in my stomach wasn't just about the prospect of an interview, with its ridiculous staged sermon and po-faced questions. 'Can you give me an example of some difficult situation that you have faced in your ministry and how you have dealt with it?' I imagined myself laughing at that question, and my interviewers staring back, unimpressed. The long train journey felt like a trip into some future loneliness, exile even. Would the interview bring up the subject of Occupy, I wondered? Perhaps just a glancing mention, a nod to the elephant in the room. The official Church line was that there wasn't an official Church line. Officially, I hadn't blotted my copybook. After all, I had been shortlisted for this new job. And publicly there had been a fair amount of backslapping and congratulations on doing the right thing, even from the top. Yet I could just feel the shadowy presence of those whispered conversations in the Athenaeum that spoke of betrayal and of not really being one of us. A number of colleagues had stopped talking to me. One priest – previously a friend – cut me dead in the street, my greeting to him apparently inaudible. He walked by, face fixed in a thousand-yard stare. I had broken ranks. Let down the team. All I had had to do was dress up and shut up. I had proved to be pretty rubbish at both. Over the last few weeks, the darkness within had begun to take root. And it was becoming all-consuming.

I arrived at Liverpool Lime Street station a couple of hours before the interview. I found a coffee shop and lit up another cigarette. I should have been reading my interview notes, but instead I sat back and watched people passing in and out of the station. I drifted into daydreaming mode, my mind set in neutral, retreating into the comforting ether. Then it came to me – at first as little more than a passing thought that I could easily have allowed to drift over into the forgotten. But something about that thought flagged itself up as having significance. Something spiked my curiosity. I did, in fact, have one extremely tenuous link with Liverpool – a long time ago. The connection was a man called Samuel Friedeberg.

Great-uncle Sam was the younger brother of my great-grandfather Louis. For over forty years, from 1891 to 1932, Samuel had been the Minister of the Liverpool Old Hebrew synagogue on Princes Road in Toxteth. He was a part of my blurred family backstory. The reason he had sometimes appeared in conversation was that, coming from an entirely secular family, and with little religious observance in even my grandparents' generation, Sam was the only person my slightly puzzled parents were able to refer back to in order to explain how their son had got God. 'It's in the blood,' was my mother's rather irritating explanation. I have always resisted that sort of biological determinism. But the synagogue was only a short walk from the cathedral. Maybe I should wander up there before the interview? Why not? The place was surely worth a look, if only to kill a little more time.

Somewhere on my shelves there is a little blue book by the Reverend Samuel Friedeberg, a rather dull-looking commentary on the book of Joshua in both English and Hebrew. In a box somewhere there is also a sepia photograph of a handsome bespectacled man with a white moustache and thick clerical collar. I always thought it odd that Jewish ministers wore clerical collars, as if they were members of the Church of England, and equally odd that they styled themselves 'Reverend' – though that was extremely common at the time. I suppose it should have been obvious that these were signs of a complex relationship with assimilation, but their significance had never fully occurred to me.

I got a taxi up from Liverpool Lime Street to Princes Road and found myself on a long, tree-lined boulevard, wide enough to feel slightly grand, full of large Victorian mansions and places of religious worship – a Welsh Presbyterian church, once the tallest building in Liverpool, the neo-Byzantine Greek Orthodox church of St Nicholas, and the synagogue. A chill wind blew down Princes Road that morning and piles of leaves swirled around my feet.

Like the Revd Samuel Friedeberg's dress and title, the synagogue is itself a study in cultural assimilation. Completed in 1874, it was built by a couple of Scottish Presbyterian brothers, William and George Audsley, who were responsible for several churches in the Liverpool area, including that very tall Welsh Presbyterian church just along the road. Despite their Nonconformist background, the brothers generally built in the elaborate Gothic Revival style, which may be why Princes Road, a Grade 1-listed gem of a synagogue, looks so remarkably like a church. Synagogue architecture often adopts the forms of the vernacular. But this synagogue felt shockingly Christian. The bimah was clearly more of a pulpit than a traditional stage. And with its deep red carpet and polished wooden pews, it had more in common with Pugin than with Palestine.

In its glory days, the synagogue on Princes Road was the 'cathedral' to the respectable Liverpool Jewry, those who had prospered in the fields of business and politics – families like the Lewises, who owned the well-known department store in Liverpool city centre, and the Samuels, founders of the H. Samuel jewellery chain. In 1909, Herbert Samuel – or to give him his full title, Viscount Samuel of Mount Carmel and Toxteth – became a Cabinet minister in the Asquith government and eventually the first High Commissioner of the British Mandate of Palestine. He was the first Jew to rule over the historic land of Israel for 2,000 years. These days his is the name of the main street that runs alongside the beach in Tel Aviv. These were the circles in which Revd Samuel Friedeberg moved: respectable, middle to upper class, and highly assimilated.

3.

The Friedebergs had made their way to Britain during the reign of George I. They arrived from northern Germany and settled in Portsmouth's developing Jewish community sometime after 1720, drawn by the coronation of a sympathetic Hanoverian to the English throne and by the promise of work that had been created by an expansion of the naval dockyards. Decades of repeated wars and war scares made Portsmouth into a huge ship-building, ship-maintaining and provisioning site. War creates jobs, and David Friedeberg arrived in England to find work.

It was only sixty or so years since Jews had been readmitted to England following 350 years of banishment. From 1290, when Edward I had expelled all Jews from England, to some point towards the end of the seventeenth century, Jews were officially not welcome in this country, banished as enemies of the state. Their readmission is often dated to Cromwell's passionate advocacy of the Jewish cause at a special conference held to discuss the matter in Whitehall in 1655, though this date is mostly symbolic.

The translation of the Bible into English, combined with the development of the printing press, opened up the Hebrew Scriptures to a non-Jewish audience as never before. With this new-found freedom to read the Scriptures outside the interpretative control of the Roman Church, they began to be understood in very different ways. Following the Reformation, the Old Testament in particular was mined by all shades of political opinion for support. In the absence of the Pope's imprimatur, the Reformation monarchs, particularly Elizabeth I, reached out to the rhetoric of the Davidic kings, inevitably Solomon, to describe and justify themselves. In complete contrast, the revolutionaries of the English Civil War found justification for turning the world upside down in the writings of the prophets and apocalyptic literature, especially the book of Daniel. These revolutionaries would adopt Hebrew names – Jeremiah, Hezekiah, Ezekiel, Obadiah, Amos – and think of themselves as the chosen, fighting the final battle between good and evil at the end of the world. Cromwell believed that the conversion of the Jews to Christianity was a necessary precursor to the second coming of Christ, and the final rule of the godly.

But Cromwell's attempt to readmit Jews in 1655 was only partially successful. Forced to back down by a powerful alliance of the Church and the city, Cromwell allowed a sort of informal permission to pertain, with Jews gradually trickling back with indeterminate status. In the late seventeenth and early eighteenth centuries, wealthier Jews – mostly Sephardic – began increasingly to arrive in London, with many of the poorer ones settling in places like Portsmouth, which was to become the oldest and, for a while, the largest Jewish community outside London. The Friedebergs were among the first generations of Ashkenazi Jews to settle back in this country, which means that they are one of the oldest Jewish families in England.

4.

Portsmouth was a tough place, even by eighteenth-century standards – 'a Gomorrah', as one clerk in the Navy Pay Office described it in 1728; and 'easily one of the roughest towns in eighteenth-century England', according to the historian Jessica Warner. War may have created the jobs, but it also fuelled a distrust of foreigners in general and Jews in particular. A common suspicion was that they were agents of the enemy, and that they were exploiting the brave servicemen of the armed forces for private profit. 'Nor war nor wisdom yields our Jews delight,' wrote the clergyman and poet George Crabbe in 1810, 'They will not study, and they dare not fight.'

The Friedebergs made their living in the narrow streets of Portsmouth Point, close by the gates of the dockyard. In the back of various low-rent dwellings they put together cheap clothes and blankets and sewed buttons on uniforms. They would occasionally branch out into general trade, and even into a bit of metal-dealing, but it was little more than peddling. The rag trade was their core business. Louis's and

Samuel's dad, Mark (born 1832), is described on the census as a 'slop seller' living in the notorious White's Row – slops being cheap clothing.

The name Mark is curious because it is not a Jewish name at all. It's a Christian name, with Roman origins. So why would his parents choose such a name? As you will come to see in the course of this book, name-changing is a familiar theme in my family. It was Mark's parents' generation that first began this tradition. Mark's father was born Moses Friedeberg (in Portsmouth about 1785) and then changed his name to Morris. Mark's uncle was born Mordechai Friedeberg and also changed his name to Mark (declared bankrupt in 1811). Mordechai's wife started life as Bilhah and ended up as Elizabeth. The most obvious explanation for these name changes is that they were a response to antisemitism, an attempt to blend in, to hide.

Of course, changing the name from the Jewish Mordechai to the Christian Mark is freighted with a very particular significance. Mordechai is famous to Jews the world over as the hero of the biblical book of Esther, a man who bravely saved his co-religionists, who were exiled in ancient Persia, by defeating a murderous plot let by the Jew-hating Harman. During Purim, Jews celebrate this story with triangular poppy-seed pastries and fancy dress. The Friedebergs must have known that changing one's name from a hero of Jewish resistance to the first evangelist of the New Testament was hardly in the spirit of Purim. But this must have been their defence against Portsmouth's often hostile culture.

As the historian Tony Kushner has demonstrated, one can glimpse something of a common attitude towards Jews living in and around naval seaports by looking at the cheap novels of the post-Napoleonic era. Here, the brave and honest English seaman is commonly depicted as being ripped off by unscrupulous Jews. This familiar trope of the port Jew, made famous by Shakespeare's Shylock on the Rialto in Venice, gives some insight into the level of popular prejudice that the Friedebergs would have encountered. The novelist Matthew Henry Barker (1790–1846), for instance, who wrote under the pseudonym 'the Old Sailor', may not have been a writer of any great literary distinction, but his sea tales were extremely popular – a precursor of the much more accomplished Hornblower books – and full of vile antisemitic stereotypes. Take his novel *Jem Bunt: A Tale of the Land and the Ocean* (1841) which specifically features Portsmouth Point, where the Friedebergs lived:

> The Point was famous for the dwellings of those kind-hearted children of Israel, who supplied the wants of the seamen at the moderate interest of about 500 per cent. Talk of your London Jews – keen as they are – a Point Jew would have cheated a dozen of them in an hour. The sea-line of this neck of land was prepared as a fortification, and its semi-circular arches used to remind me of an enormous mouse trap.

Later, the novel describes the fun that the sailors had in hiding a knuckle of ham inside the character Nathan's coat. This recalls an actual event as described by Jessica Warner: in 1781 'Israel Abraham and his wife were eating dinner when Henry Fisher opened the door of their house and threw in a dead pig, causing Abraham's wife, who was pregnant at the time, to be "greatly terrified".'

Throughout the novel, the mendacity of the shifty Jew is contrasted with the straightforward honest decency of the native seafarer. Jem Bunt concludes: 'The English are a brave and intelligent people when dealing with an open enemy; but they suffer themselves to be too easily gulled and deluded by pretended friends among themselves, and who only use them as tools and instruments to secure their own aggrandisement.'

If this was the sort of thing that the Friedeburgs had to contend with, it is little wonder they sought the camouflage of a Christian-sounding name. And it was not just from the working class that they would have encountered antisemitic prejudice. During the 1840s, *The Times* ran a series of high-profile horror stories about how Jewish slop sellers were pushing young English women to work for starvation wages, or forcing them into prostitution. This turned into something of a moral panic among the chattering classes, with Jews being widely blamed for the very conditions of poverty that they themselves had to struggle in.

It was a hard life, with the English victory over Napoleon – and the subsequent scaling back of the navy – destroying much of the local economy. In 1849, when Mark was seventeen, a thousand people died from a cholera epidemic that spread through the cramped and dirty streets of Portsmouth Point. One doctor described conditions as 'deficient in every requisite to health, comfort, and cleanliness'. Crime was widespread. Mark and his wife, Amalia, wanted more than this for their children. Soon an opportunity presented itself through their local synagogue.

In 1850, the Chief Rabbi of Britain and the British Empire made his first ever visit to the town. Nathan Marcus HaKohen Adler was old school, originating in Hanover like the Friedebergs, and coming from a long line of rabbis and theologians, many of whom had served with distinction in the ghettos of continental Europe. Appointed following the formation of a breakaway reform congregation in London, Dr Adler was especially concerned to unify the national Jewish community around the Chief Rabbinate. He was thus the first Chief Rabbi to tour the country.

His five-day trip to Portsmouth was a huge success. The mayor and city dignitaries dined with him in grand style. A band from HMS *Victory* played in his honour, then later rowed him out to the ship for a tour. And the Ladies Guild presented him with a fine silver tea service. The eighteen-year-old Mark, scratching out a living in the slums, would have seen all this and registered the opportunity it presented – if not for him, then perhaps for his children. What Mark could not have guessed was that his future son, Samuel, and the Chief Rabbi's son, Hermann, would one day be friends.

5.

Among those who managed to escape the Portsmouth ghetto was a young man called Lewis Aria, a trader who chanced his arm and boarded a ship to the West Indies, where he made his fortune – a proportion of which he left to set up a Rabbinical college in his old home town. 'Every student will receive such yearly stipend or allowance not being less than £20 or greater than £30 as the Trustees see fit' was the stipulation for Aria College. 'Every Candidate must previously to admission furnish evidence of his good character, freedom from offensive or infectious disease, and a knowledge of English and Hebrew.'

This was Samuel's way out. In a meeting recorded on 6 July 1876, in the Queens Lane synagogue in the street right next to where the Friedebergs had lived for around 150 years, they 'resolved that Samuel Friedeberg, a native of Portsea, be elected as a student, having previously with his father signed the bond and declaration'. Samuel was only fourteen. In the chair for that meeting was Hermann Adler, the Chief Rabbi's son and later his successor.

The curriculum at Aria College says quite a lot about the breadth of education the Jewish community felt their future leaders should receive. Alongside courses on Hebrew grammar, Rashi and the Pentateuch, the Mishnah and Isaiah (Friedeberg was 'very good', Hermann Adler writes in his report), they also studied English history and German grammar ('Friedeberg's pronunciation is faulty') and Latin grammar and algebra.

For those who looked back to continental Jewry for theological inspiration, faulty German pronunciation was a problem. But for others, who wanted their religious leaders to reflect a more English sensibility, it was a positive advantage. Samuel and his father may have fallen out with the trustees of the college over Mark's wish for Samuel to continue his studies at the more prestigious Jews' College in London, but flunking out of Aria didn't seem to hold him back. In his twenties, Sam was employed as a Minister of Religion by the Newcastle Synagogue, preaching to the major Jewish populations of Gateshead and all over the north east. And then, in 1891, still under thirty, he was appointed to the prestigious pulpit of Princes Road.

Far from being a problem, Samuel's British ancestry was, in fact, a condition of his employment in Liverpool. The Braham Lectureship, by which the leadership of the Liverpool synagogue was to be financed, was funded by a bequest from a wealthy gold merchant called James Braham. Born Zachariah Abrahams in Plymouth in 1811, the anglicized Braham not only jettisoned the first and last letters of his surname but also left an annual endowment of £13,000 to fund two positions at the synagogue on the strict condition that the senior appointee had British parents. The unfortunate incumbent minister, the Revd Joseph Polack, didn't have British parents and resigned – or was pressured to resign – making way for my great-uncle Sam to take up his job.

When Samuel arrived in Liverpool in 1891, he was (unlike the poor Revd Polack) already a fifth-generation English Jew, and he had already done a pretty good job disguising the fact that his father had been a slop seller from the back-streets of Portsmouth Point. But it wasn't just the conditions of the Braham bequest that helped Samuel obtain his prestigious new position. In 1890 the old Chief Rabbi, Nathan Adler, died. His son, Samuel's college mentor, Hermann Adler, was chosen to succeed him, though he had already been standing in for his sick father, and thus effectively doing his job, for a number of years. Samuel was precisely the sort of cleric that the new Chief Rabbi was keen to promote, a perfect disciple of the so-called Minhag Anglia.

The Minhag Anglia – or the English tradition – was a specific way in which nineteenth-century Anglo-Jewry chose to acculturate their faith within the British context. Its origins are earlier than the Chief Rabbinate of Nathan Adler – arguably, it goes back to the very invention of the Chief Rabbinate itself, which was an innovation in Judaism and echoed the role of the Archbishop of Canterbury. But it was with Nathan Adler that the Ashkenazi Synagogue had begun its transformation into a Jewish version of the establishment Church of England. Under Nathan Adler, Jewish clergy began to be styled 'Reverend' and 'Very Reverend' and adopted the use of banns and clerical collars. The singers who led the services, the Chazanim, became precentors, and the lay leaders of the synagogue became wardens, just like church wardens in the Church of England. When Hermann Adler took over from his father, this anglicization accelerated, with the Chief Rabbi going so far as to adopt a suggestion from the Bishop of Bath and Wells that he should wear bishop's gaiters.

The whole expectation of upper-middle-class decorum in worship was a novelty. Like the Church of England, the Minhag Anglia emphasized a certain formality in divine worship, rejecting as anarchic the boisterous sort of synagogue worship that immigrant Jews were bringing with them from the Russian Empire. Hermann Adler encouraged a Jewish version of the Anglican Prayer Book – the so-called 'Singer's Prayer Book' – and introduced the practice of a weekly sermon. In August 1886 a letter of complaint appeared in the *Jewish Chronicle* from an American who had been refused a decent seat at a London synagogue. Not only that, but he was not permitted to read from the Torah because he wouldn't wear a top hat. It was 'remarkable evidence that Jews are only too ready to follow the ways of the nations among whom they dwell', the American grumbled.

In 1871, the *Jewish Chronicle* summed up the overriding philosophy of the Minhag Anglia: 'We Jews of England are not only in England; we are of England. We are not only British Jews, we are Jewish Englishmen. It is our boast and our pleasure and our pride that we can claim and fulfil the duties of Britons without sacrificing our Judaism, without neglecting its observances and without abandoning its sacred hopes.' Others were less kind towards the philosophy of the Minhag Anglia. Rabbi Hermann Adler was once described by a newspaper columnist as 'the willing captive of the gilded gentry'. The accusation was commonly levelled – especially by Jewish immigrants – that English Jews had been sucking up to the establishment for too long. From this perspective, they had traded in their historic faith for an invitation to dine in posh London clubs and – for one or two – a seat in the House of Lords.

The Minhag Anglia was also criticized for neglecting the scholarly dimension of Jewish life. Indeed, most congregations of the United Synagogue did not think it especially important for their ministers to have received the sort of theological instruction that would have made them suitable for rabbinic ordination. Training at Jews' College, for example, was specifically designed to create pastors and community leaders – again like the C of E – rather than experts in the law.

I had always presumed that Samuel was ordained a rabbi. But it turns out he wasn't. Being a Jewish 'Reverend' wasn't the same thing. Congregations like Liverpool's wanted an urbane public figure who would enhance the respectability of their community. They felt they had little need of a scholar who would instruct them on the complexity of the Talmud. Indeed, throughout the nineteenth-century Chief Rabbinate of both father and son Adler there were to be no other home-grown English rabbis over whom they were Chief. One rabbi was deemed enough for the whole country. The Adlers, it was said, were generals without an army. And whilst immigrant Jews from the Continent regularly disparaged the (to them) very confusing idea of Jewish reverends and England's paucity of rabbis, the centralizing instincts of the Adlers meant that they refused to share authority. As a consequence, and like much of the soft-focus, low-grade Anglicanism that it copied, the Jewish Reverends concerned themselves with community work rather than anything more erudite. A divine calling was understood primarily in terms of pastoral care.

Thus in his 'Four Epistles to the Jews of England', the Romanian scholar Solomon Schechter complains that the Jewish minister was 'rapidly losing touch with the venerable Rabbi of Jewish tradition, whose chief office was to teach and to *learn* Torah'. He goes on, despairingly:

. . . most of his energies are directed towards acquiring the amount of secular learning necessary for the obtaining of a

University degree, whilst in his capacity as full Reverend, he is expected to divide his time between the offices of cantor, prayer, preacher, book-keeper, debt-collector, almoner, and social agitator. No leisure is left to him to enable him to increase his scanty stock of Hebrew knowledge acquired in his undergraduate days. Occasionally rumour spreads about some minister, that he neglects his duty to his congregation, through his being strictly addicted to Jewish learning. But such rumours often turn out to be sheer malice . . .

Such a thing could easily have been said about Samuel. He was a man of his moment, precisely the sort of minister that Braham and the younger Adler approved of: serious, conservative, cautious, public-spirited, keen on secular learning – and without the trace of a foreign accent. At the end of his forty-one-year ministry, and feted by the British establishment, his citation for an honorary MA bestowed on him by Liverpool University described Samuel Friedeberg thus:

[F]or more than 40 years the learned active minister of an important Liverpool synagogue and in Jewish literature he is an author and editor of high reputation. But his service has always extended beyond the borders of his own community and more than one of our philanthropic and social organizations has profited from his wisdom, his experiences and his helpful energy. He is still a working member of the Liverpool education committee. In honouring him today, we offer no more than his due to one who has helped make our city better than he found it. In conferring this degree we seek to honour the minister, the scholar and the man of affairs.

He had done his mentors proud.

But for all Samuel's success in Liverpool, it was events abroad that kept on intruding into his carefully arranged life – not least the events surrounding his change of name. By the time of this citation from Liverpool University, Revd Samuel Friedeberg had become the Revd Samuel Frampton.

6.

Samuel Friedeberg's tenure at Princes Road spanned one of the most traumatic periods in Jewish history. Though Jewish life in England was relatively safe and, for some, increasingly prosperous, the situation over in the east of continental Europe was completely different. In 1881, the assassination of Alexander II released a tidal wave of antisemitic violence throughout the Russian Empire, where the vast majority of the world's Jews had come to settle. In May 1882, the so-called May Laws were passed, forcing Jews living in villages to resettle in towns, cancelling their right to hold mortgages and prohibiting them from working on Christian holy days. This was just the beginning. Soon, quotas were imposed on the number of Jews that could attend school or university. Jews were expelled from government jobs. Between 1881 and 1914, 2 million Jews left the Russian Empire; 100,000 of them came to London and 4,000 to Liverpool. This influx of Jewish refugees was to lead to Britain's first great moral panic over immigration and the subsequent Alien Act of 1905, an attempt to establish immigration controls.

The social and cultural distance between the newcomers and the established Minhag Anglia Jewish community made for a complex relationship and threatened the hard-earned respectability that Samuel Friedeberg and his congregation had done so much to cultivate. The newcomers were generally Yiddish-speaking, more religious and poor. 'The Russian Jew is among us, but not of us,' wrote the *Jewish Chronicle* in 1884. 'His dress, his food, his habits, his speech, his mode of prayer are as near as possible here what they were in the half-civilized village in which he was born.'

The contrast between these Russian 'village' Jews and the upwardly mobile middle-class English Jews, which now included Samuel, could hardly have been greater. The long-standing Jewish community at Princes Road had been the first to allow synagogue preaching in English, back in the early nineteenth century. Unlike the new Jews pouring off the boats, they were urbane and liberal, perhaps even lax in their religious practice. Many of the Princes Road community were not overly concerned with the strict observance of the rules of kashrut and Shabbat, and intermarriage was becoming increasingly common. Herbert Samuel abandoned his religious belief at Oxford. Like Samuel Friedeberg, respectable established Jews were keen to be seen as English Jews, with particular emphasis on the English bit. The Samuels and the Friedebergs, with their waistcoats and top hats, lived in a totally different world from the boot-wearing, violin-playing peasants from Odessa or Łódź who were crammed into the Oceanic Hotel on Liverpool's Duke Street or around the train station.

Writing in the *Liverpool Review* in 1899, one columnist graded the city's Jews thus:

> To begin with at the lowest, there is the comparatively newly imported foreign Jew. Then there is the naturalized progeny of the foreign Jew, after these came the Jews of whose foreign descent is hazed in several forgotten generations, and the last and anything but least, especially as far as the ego of the individual is concerned, is the English Jew. This latter

specimen votes Liberal or Tory, reverences roast beef and keeps Christmastide.

This described my father's family to a tee.

Economic and class distinctions effectively excluded the refugees from membership of the Princes Road synagogue, so the newcomers set up their own cheaper and more informal house groups that eventually developed into full-blown synagogues, draining members from Princes Road. The Revd Friedeberg complained that these new places of worship lacked a proper sense of decorum. Or, to put it another way, they weren't sufficiently like the Jewish/Church of England hybrid that his synagogue had become.

7.

But something much more threatening was also on the horizon: the war. In 1915, a German U-boat torpedoed the RMS *Lusitania* off the coast of Ireland, en route from New York to Liverpool. What had once been the biggest ship in the world went down in eighteen minutes, causing the deaths of 1,198 passengers and crew, many of whom were from Liverpool, where the ship was registered. Within days, anti-German riots had spread across the city and from there throughout the country. On 11 May 1915, the *Liverpool Courier* described it thus:

The disaster to the *Lusitania*, in which helpless non-combatants were foully murdered, has affected Liverpool in particular. By one coward blow hundreds of homes in the city have been bereft. Can there be any wonder that among the less disciplined classes, who have had to freely sacrifice their menfolk on the battlefield, the feeling of bitter enmity against the Germans should be exacerbated beyond restraint? From the streets wherein dwelt the sailors and firemen who were murdered by the Germans who torpedoed the *Lusitania* have gone crowds of people who, in their passionate resentment against all things Teutonic, have not been able to distinguish between friends and foe.

This inability of some native Scousers to distinguish Germans from other foreign European immigrants meant that many Jews were targeted and beaten up and their shop windows smashed. The increasing suspicion of 'foreign Jews' wasn't just confined to the mob either – the Defence of the Realm Act 1914 had raised the spectre of an enemy within, with many non-naturalized aliens, including Liverpool Jews, being shipped off to internment camps on the Isle of Man. This was profoundly unfair, of course. At the outbreak of the war Liverpool's Jews had been overwhelmingly enthusiastic about signing up to join the army, and thirteen of the synagogue's 113 volunteers were killed in the trenches.

Even so, as elsewhere, there were protesters against the war in the Jewish community – not least among formerly Russian Jews, who were understandably reluctant to take up arms alongside their former Tsarist persecutors. But it was the contentious objection of one of Samuel's close colleagues, the junior Braham lecturer and pacifist the Revd John Harris, that caused particular consternation in the community. Objecting to the war, Harris could easily have been charged under the Defence of the Realm Act and sent to prison, alongside more prominent conscientious objectors like Bertrand Russell. In circumstances in which the Jewish community was under continual suspicion, that could have been disastrous – and so Samuel sacked him. Loyalty to the crown trumped loyalty to his colleague.

Something else also added to Samuel's sense of cultural

insecurity: the hotly debated question of Zionism that was increasingly causing division among the settled Jewish community. The First Zionist Congress had been convened by Theodor Herzl in 1897 in Switzerland and was highly controversial among English Jews.

In 1898, the Chief Rabbi of the British Empire, Hermann Adler, Samuel's mentor, fiercely condemned Zionism as incompatible with Judaism:

> 'My brothers! I look at this movement with worry in my heart, since I see it as opposed to the Torah of Hashem and to politics. There is a great danger involved in it. That is why I don't see in it the great quality of love of Zion ... The hope which the Torah implanted in our hearts cannot lead us into intrigues, diplomatic manoeuvres, rebellion or fighting in order to inherit the land of our fathers and found a kingdom there. On the contrary, our faith teaches us to seek the welfare of the nations under whose protection we dwell, to take part in their national efforts and work for their success, and to wait silently for the day when the words of the prophets will be fulfilled.'

The Chief Rabbi was not alone in his hostility to the Zionist dream. For many, Zionism came to be seen as a test of loyalty to the crown. And initially at least, Samuel was suspicious of it, only gradually becoming converted to the cause. In 1917, in the run-up to the Balfour Declaration, the Princes Road community debated a motion: that the foundation of a Jewish state would 'prejudicially affect the position of such Jews as are members of the British nation'. The motion was defeated, but only by thirty-nine votes to thirty. It was a close-run thing.

In 1916, on the silver jubilee of his appointment at Princes Road, and riding high in society, Samuel Friedeberg changed his name to Frampton. It was the year after the *Lusitania* riots and the year before the Balfour Declaration – and it was an unequivocal statement. He may have come round to the Zionist cause after much initial hostility, but he wanted to make it absolutely clear that his primary loyalty was to Britain. The name change was intended to seal it.

I knew nothing of any of this the day I went for my interview and got out of the taxi on Princes Road. I knew little more about great-uncle Samuel than his name. It was a fresh January morning and the trees were exposed, stripped back to the wood. The synagogue was locked and no lights were on. Perhaps it was only a museum now. I half thought about turning back, but eventually banged on the door with no real expectation of anyone being there. A caretaker answered the door and I explained my interest. She led me into a side room. I wandered around, not knowing what to look for. But there, on the wall and in pride of place, was a large oil painting of the Revd Samuel Frampton. I stood staring up at his distinguished face, searching out his features to catch some family resemblance. I could find little in common between his face and mine, nor with that of my father and grandfather. But, however distant, he was still family. This is where I came from.

And then, for some curious reason that I could not understand, something gave way inside me. Unexpectedly, inexplicably, foolishly, I left the synagogue and sat down at the side of the road, lit up a cigarette and cried. For a good twenty minutes I wept, without really knowing why. I'm not sure I had cried properly since the whole Occupy thing. Maybe the shock of it all had kept the tears at bay. Then, for some extraordinary reason, this large oil painting of Revd Frampton unleashed a flood of emotion.

The more I read about Samuel – this ghost that had so suddenly confronted me – the more archives I looked into,

74

the more I tried to bring him alive, the more the problem became obvious to me. I didn't belong anywhere. I was caught in between – not Jewish, and now not a part of the Anglican club that my family had done so much to become a part of. Disraeli once described himself as 'the blank page between the Old Testament and the New'. Queen Victoria had no idea what he meant. But I do. Like him, I feel myself between two worlds.

Later that morning I go to the interview. It doesn't go well. I answer the questions as if I don't want the job. I am not chosen.

8.

I am Giles Fraser, son of Anthony, son of Harold, son of Louis, son of Mark, son of Morris, son of Jacob, son of Judah, son of David – all English Jews stretching back to the early eighteenth century. All Jews, that is, except for me.

Yet despite this impeccably Hebrew male heredity – crucially on my father's side – it was my non-Jewish mother who taught me the love of all things Jewish. She grew up in working-class Leicestershire, in a claustrophobic pebble-dashed council house that couldn't have been more Gentile if it tried. As goy as it gets, a friend once observed. On the walls hung those little pottery plates with improving verses from Scripture. The one in the freezing cold outside loo read: 'Prepare to meet thy God', which was always slightly disconcerting. The house had a front room kept for best that no one ever ventured into, and dark, respectable, inexpensive, lovingly polished sideboards, defended on every side by carefully maintained net curtains. It was a place turned in on itself, and a repository of secrets.

There were three residents of that unhappy museum. My desperately insecure, pint-sized, squeaky-voiced grandmother; her husband, my kind, long-suffering grandfather, who spent most of the time in hiding, down on his precious allotment; and, third, a man called Ron, who was a travelling salesman that my grandfather had brought home from work one day and who ended up staying for ever, sharing more than my grandfather's generous offer of table and shelter. Growing up, my mother would lie in bed at night listening to her mother carrying on with the salesman downstairs and scolding her husband for his working clothes and muddy shoes.

But it wasn't just the arrangement with Ron that had cut my grandmother off from the village and the rest of her family. Many years later, in 2012, a letter arrived out of the blue, addressed to my mother, handwritten in Italian. Not knowing any Italian, my mum took it to a neighbour for translation. Within half an hour the neighbour was back on the doorstep with some surprising news. My grandmother had been dead for several years, which was probably just as well. My mother's younger brother was actually her half-brother, the letter explained. It turns out that my grandmother had had an affair with one of the Italian prisoners of war who worked on the local farm, and she fell pregnant. Apparently he was not the only prisoner she shared her affections with. She was friendly with Germans as well as Italians. The village knew, and they ostracized her. That was why the house had always felt lonely and besieged.

My mother dreamed of escape, of a life beyond that hideously tense *ménage à trois* with its whispered confidences and moralistic church-going camouflage. Running away to become a nurse, she met my father: his background was north London, expensive school, RAF officer and Jewish.

In truth, she didn't have very much idea about what being Jewish meant. It was her word for a dream, an escape route to something more glamorous, urban, exotic and international. Her first impression of her in-laws was that they shopped at Harrods, said 'darling' all the time and, most impressive of all, had carpet in the loo. It was a front, of course, but she didn't know that at the time. The important thing was that it was a world somewhere beyond small-village Leicestershire.

Later in life, my mother would fill the house with the smell of cold fried fish and insist that the values of the family and table were quintessentially Jewish. To her sons, she would extol the virtues of Jewish men; they were cleverer and sexier. This was the joke. I had a Jewish father who pretended he wasn't and a non-Jewish mother who pretended she was.

9.

Louis Friedeberg often followed the lead of his more successful younger brother. The year after Revd Samuel Friedeberg became Revd Samuel Frampton, Louis Friedeberg became Louis Fraser. By the time he had changed his name, Louis was already married with two boys, one of whom was my grandfather, Harold. The teenage Harold was also obliged to change his surname to Fraser, meaning that my father was the first in the family to have been born with the Fraser surname. Growing up, I assumed that the Fraser name went much further back; that it had changed so long ago it was hardly worth mentioning. But knowing that my father was the first-born of the Frasers made my name feel superficial, made up – almost a lie. I have never discovered the reason Louis chose Fraser rather than Frampton. As far as I can tell, it was an identity plucked out of thin air.

Unlike that of his older brother, the details of Louis's Portsmouth education are unknown, but by 1883, when he was twenty-four, Louis had been appointed as clerk to the Industrial Committee of the Board of Guardians for the Relief of the Jewish Poor and had moved up to London. The Jewish Board of Guardians, as it was better known, was established in 1859 by the great and the good of the three largest Ashkenazi synagogues in London, and funded partly by the Rothschild family, to provide welfare for the increasing number of destitute Jews who had begun to arrive in the East End of London from Eastern Europe. The early records of the board reveal some heartbreaking cases of desperation, especially those of abandoned children left by their parents at the quayside as they made their way on to America, the new Promised Land.

For all the heartache and poverty it had to deal with, the board wasn't keen on encouraging handouts. Its ethos was 'to avoid any form of aid that might pauperize the recipient or create passive dependency'. To this end, Louis was engaged to arrange apprenticeships for young Jewish men and women with good Jewish companies that would give them a trade and would understand their need for Sabbath observance. And it was whilst touring the capital looking for sympathetic employers that Louis met his future father-in-law, the up-and-coming entrepreneur Jacob Kempner, who had not long arrived off the boat from Poland with his daughter Rose, my great-grandmother. They were immigrants, yes, but not like the ones Samuel was so threatened by in Liverpool or those whom the Board of Guardians had been set up to care for. The Kempners were successful.

Despite all the political upheaval following the Russian persecution of European Jewry, it can't have been an easy decision for the Kempners to leave for London. Jacob and his wife, Gupta, had five children, and none of them spoke a word of English. Moreover, Łódź had become a prosperous place, its textile industry having taken advantage of disruption to the American production of cotton during the American Civil War. In the second half of the nineteenth century Łódź became known as the Polish Manchester, with smoky chimneys and large brick factories. Roughly a third of the population was Jewish; many of them poor, but some, like the Kempners, increasingly well-to-do.

Jacob's brother, Herman, had decided to stick it out and stay in Łódź. Why leave when things were going so well? A picture taken of him by a society photographer in the early 1900s shows a prosperous-looking man in a smart suit and handlebar moustache. He had risen up from a master tailor to be the manager of the Zieger textile mill. His family lived in a fine house on the main square in the city, across from the famously beautiful Stara synagogue. Built in a Moorish style, containing 1,500 seats and thirty-six stunning Torah scrolls, the Stara synagogue was one of the architectural gems of European Jewry. Herman and his wife were not prepared to leave behind their home and all that they had worked for. But it was Jacob who made the right decision: to leave. The German army occupied Łódź in September 1939 and burned down the Stara synagogue within two months of arriving. Most of the town's Jews – both rich and poor – perished of starvation in the Łódź ghetto or were transported to concentration camps and the gas chambers. All of Herman's children died in the ghetto.

Jacob Kempner set himself up in Hackney, bringing with him the skills and entrepreneurial energy of the Łódź manufacturing tradition. The first of his shoe shops, Jacob Kempner and Sons, Boot and Shoe Manufacturers, was established opposite the Hackney Empire on Mare Street. Soon he was operating out of properties on Paragon Road and Well Street as well. Jacob Kempner left £5,602 to his son on his death – over £600,000 in today's money. He did pretty well for himself.

My great-grandparents, Louis Friedeberg and Rose Kempner, were married in the Dalston synagogue on Poets Road in north London on 20 June 1894. The synagogue was demolished in the 1970s to make way for an ugly block of Islington council flats. It is the place where I feel the ghosts most strongly. Nothing on the corner of that quiet suburban street evokes any memory of the place of worship that used to be there, the high days and holidays that were celebrated, or the sermons or the marriages. Standing on Poets Road, I find it almost impossible to imagine the life that went on here before these flats were built. It is as if it had never happened.

But I do have a couple of photographs of the place. The building was a typical example of Victorian synagogue architecture, with similar proportions to that of a mid-sized Victorian church. It was built of plain red brick, with horizontal stone bands, and two arched doorways. Inside, it had a high roof and galleries with supporting classical columns, painted to look like marble, facing each other across a black-and-white stone floor. At the east end, the ark containing the Torah scrolls looked dark and scary, all heavy wood and velvet coverings. The Hebrew script of the Ten Commandments, set over the recess of the ark, was one of the few references that this was a Middle Eastern religion. Despite the large brass light fittings, the lighting was low. And given the number of cast-iron radiators, so was the heating. Photographs show the men and women wrapped up in large coats and hats, even during services. It wasn't anything like the magnificent Stara synagogue back in Łódź. Nothing close.

Even so, Jewish weddings at the end of the nineteenth

century were often glamorous occasions, with many Jewish brides enthusiastically adopting the fashion of wearing large white wedding gowns. The men would stand proudly in their suits and waistcoats, most of them with a fine sprouting of facial hair. It was another twenty-plus years before the celebrated Whitechapel photographer Boris Bennett would merge the look of the London Jewish wedding with that of Hollywood glamour, dressing up secretaries to look like film stars, even building his own theatrical sets. But long before that many Jewish weddings were highly aspirational occasions, lavish and expensive, reflecting more the dreams of the couple than their financial reality. The wedding was intended as a statement of where they were heading, not where they had come from.

I imagine my great-grandparents standing on that black-and-white checked floor, under the chuppah. I imagine Louis waiting nervously, being supported by his brother, who had come down from Liverpool to take the service. I think of Rose, still learning about her new country, and not knowing what this new life was to be. I think of them smashing the glass and remembering the first destruction of the Temple and singing from Psalm 137, 'If I forget thee, O Jerusalem . . . let my tongue cleave to the roof of my mouth.' From all that I can tell, theirs was a love match. Their marriage was to be long and happy.

On that wedding day the Friedebergs and the Kempners had much to celebrate. Mark Friedeberg was sixty-two. In his lifetime he had seen his family climb out of Portsmouth Point and find respectability in London and Liverpool. With his eldest boy getting married to the daughter of a relatively prosperous shoe manufacturer, he must have felt the days of being abused and disrespected by Portsmouth's drunken sailors were far behind them all. The year 1894 was also the year Marks and Spencer was founded. English Jews were going places.

Assisting Samuel with the wedding service was the incumbent of the Dalston synagogue, Samuel's opposite number, the Revd Moses Hyamson. They were both proponents of the Minhag Anglia. Eventually a distinguished New York rabbi, Revd Hyamson became famous. And because of this, he later published a number of his sermons, some from his time at Dalston. One in particular caught my attention – given on the death of Queen Victoria in 1901:

> Today, the voice of lamentation is heard in the land. Every head is bowed, every heart is heavy, every eye dim with tears ... the King of Terrors ... [has] snatched a flower of rarest worth ... Farewell, beautiful soul! Thy arduous labours have earned thee repose.

Revd Hyamson's sermon rehearsed the ways in which many Jews had prospered during Victoria's reign.

> We Jews never shall forget that it was during her reign that we lost the Ghetto bend and learned to stand erect. Sixty-four years ago, the Jew, even in this land of enlightenment, was a barely tolerated alien. He was excluded from the boon of a liberal University education. He was ineligible for State Service. He was debarred from Parliamentary representation. What a marvellous change has taken place in two short generations, thanks largely to the good example of good Queen Victoria. Nine years after her accession, a Jew received the honour of a Baronetcy ... Twelve years later, success finally crowned the efforts of the City of London and the Borough of Greenwich to be represented by Jews in the House of Commons. In the next decade, a Jew was appointed Solicitor-General.

Little wonder well-to-do English Jewry had reason for gratitude towards Queen Victoria. And Revd Hyamson was anxious that with her departure a new era was about to dawn. 'Why this universal lament for one who had attained a hoary old age? The reason is to be found in the general feeling that the close of this gracious life closes an epoch in English history. Queen Victoria's death rings the knell of the departed century.'

I think the wedding of Louis and Rose was a high point in my family's history. I often fantasize about being there, wondering exactly how it looked and what they looked like. I have sought to dig out fragments of their lives and feel genuine excitement when something is pieced together. Just as the lament that Moses Hyamson gave for the passing of the nineteenth century also reflected the excitement that many Jews felt towards the end of the Victorian era and the hope that they would finally be accepted as peers in mainstream society, so, too, the wedding of Louis and Rose must have felt like some platform for future success and happiness. Perhaps Jews like the Friedebergs and the Kempners had finally been accepted.

10.

When my father first expressed the desire to get baptized and confirmed with the rest of his class, my grandmother drove down to his prep school to talk him out of it. She succeeded, but only temporarily. She hadn't bothered with a bar mitzvah for him, but clearly felt that baptism was going a bit too far. Some years later, when he joined the RAF, my father quietly slipped off to St Albans Abbey Church to complete the cultural job of assimilation. He got himself baptized on the quiet.

So why did my father convert? My working assumption has always been something like this: he was a small boy with a stammer and was pushed about at school, and his residual Judaism – such as it was – marked him out as different, as some sort of target. The bullying cruelties of the public-school system took him apart, then offered to make him whole again through social conformity and following the religion of the King James Bible. His wasn't really the believing-in-God type of religion. He never took all that much interest in church, even when I decided to become a priest. Mostly, I assumed, my dad just wanted the C of E stamp in his emotional passport. Growing up, he rarely went to shul and had developed little affinity with his fellow stammerer Moses. He wanted to be 'properly' English, and, to my father, that meant not being Jewish. So in one brief twenty-minute ceremony of discreet Anglican water sprinkling, he severed a connection that went back many thousands of years.

But what my dad was unable to disguise was the full-force, central-casting Golders Green Jewishness of his parents: Miriam Beckerman, a seamstress, otherwise known as Mary Baker (among several other confusing aliases) and Louis's son, Harold Fraser, an entrepreneur and gambler. One look at Harold and my dad and it would be hard to imagine they were anything other than Jewish.

I always assumed my father's decision to convert to Christianity had little to do with religious conviction and much more to do with the circumstances of his childhood. In their different ways, both of his parents were curious figures. Louis's son Harold was a combination of public school charm and West End chancer, with an eye for the ladies. He died of lung cancer in 1961, a few years before I was born. My grandmother always maintained she divorced him because he was forever dobbing out his cigar ash on her precious carpet. But, in reality, it was probably because of his infidelities. 'Guilty of adultery' was the reason given on their divorce certificate. The cigar story was just saving face. His funeral was made up of a cast of disappointed restaurateurs and glamorous unknown women, some of whom, much to my grandmother's evident disapproval, were black. 'Schwartzers' was how she described them, bitterly.

She had some reason to be bitter. They had conceived my father out of wedlock and Harold, with one marriage behind him, would eventually leave her with two young children and not a penny of support. Harold had bought a block of flats in Hampstead just before the Second World War. By the time he returned from the war, the Luftwaffe had reduced his flats to rubble. The compensation he received from the government was barely enough to pay off the mortgage. He was left with nothing. Later, he opened a bridge club in Harley Street and, inevitably, lost more money. In the last period of his life, he was always borrowing a few quid off my father, always on the verge of making a mint with some new scheme. Always losing the lot.

For my grandmother, it was a precarious existence. She made her living as a seamstress for the rich and famous, working all hours running up a dress over a weekend for her wealthy clients. Her speciality was copying couture dresses from magazines at knock-down prices. She was forever sewing, working long hours into the night. But mixing in such high-end circles meant she had to pretend. Her various addresses were always more fashionable than she had the money for. As the rent man closed in with legal demands, she would scoop up the children in the middle of the night and disappear to a new address. She did what she had to do to survive. This is probably why she had so many aliases.

My grandmother's official documents are very peculiar. There are just too many names and misdirections. Her birth certificate names her as Miriam Baker, daughter of Alfred Baker (jeweller), but also as 'Rosie Baker, late Cohen, formerly Myers'. Curiously, this same Rosie Baker, her mother, is described in her will as 'Rose Beckerman commonly known as Rose Baker'. It's all very confusing. She told us that her mother had arrived in this country from Riga, travelling on the boat third class, amid the rats.

My father's parents – apparently called Miriam Baker and Harold Fraser – were married in the Liberal Synagogue in St John's Wood in 1933. The wedding certificate describes her then as Muriel Beckerman, daughter of Simon Beckerman (tailor). Thus on the two most important official documents of her life, my grandmother has two different fathers (Alfred Baker, a jeweller, on her birth certificate and Simon Beckerman, a tailor, on her marriage certificate), and two different names (Muriel Beckerman and Miriam Baker). Perhaps this is why I knew her as Baba after the Beach Boys' song she used to sing us: 'Ba- Ba- Ba- Ba- Barbara Ann'. She was such a mystery that even I didn't use her real name. The lies had built up so high it was probably nigh on impossible even for her to distinguish fact from fiction. With Baba, one always got the impression that the truth was something of a plastic concept, made malleable by the practical realities of keeping up appearances and supporting two children on a shoestring.

When I became a priest, Baba was overjoyed. 'So proud,' she kept on repeating. Kvelling, more like. She liked that word (it's Yiddish for 'gushing with pride'). She turned up at the service in her fur coat and jewellery, desperate to join in. That was the Fraser way. Nobody thought anything of it that a sixty-year-old lady with a blue rinse would totter up for

Communion, just like everybody else, offering out her flattened palms to receive the Eucharist, glancing from side to side to make sure she was doing it right. Despite the fact that it was on her dining-room table in St John's Wood that the mohel had come to circumcise me a few days after birth, she too had given in to the Anglican thing in the end. Had she ever seen me in all my kit at St Paul's, she would have loved my red buttons. But some years before that, I took her funeral at a windswept crematorium outside Cambridge. The duty organist was understandably confused. I walked up to the desk wearing cassock, surplice, scarf and hood: standard-issue Anglican clerical garb. Then, when I opened my mouth to speak, out came the mourner's Kaddish: 'Yit'gadal v'yit'kadash sh'mei raba. . . .' This was the family secret.

It is impossible to penetrate the secrets and lies that surrounded my father's parents. But clearly, their flighty existence was a major contributing factor in my dad's desire for wanting out. A non-Jewish girl and a smart RAF officer's uniform – not to mention baptism and confirmation – were ways of drawing a line under all that emotional chaos.

For many years I think I was secretly angry with my dad for not talking about his conversion, or for being evasive about it. He wouldn't call it a conversion, and when questioned he would withdraw. Indeed, he would always maintain, defensively, 'I'm not Jewish.' The only reference I ever remember him making to being Jewish was once when I got him really annoyed by questioning his work designing weapons for British Aerospace. He shouted something at me about the need for security and used the phrase 'our people'. Then he went quiet.

For years, I presumed my father had made a purposeful act of rejection. That he had deliberately abandoned the faith of his ancestors. But the more I looked into it and exposed the family history, the more I realized it wasn't really like that. In 1942, when Hitler's bombs started raining down on London, my dad was taken out to a prep school, many miles away in the Devon countryside, for safety. He grew up wearing a blue prep-school cap with a little pale blue cross in it. His parents hadn't taken him to synagogue – even though Harold, like his father, Louis, was still a seat-holder at Golders Green synagogue. The headmaster of his school in Bideford was an old school evangelical, and so Christianity was pretty much all my father knew growing up. He didn't really convert, as such. There was no deliberate moment of apostasy, not even the baptism at St Albans. To speak of conversion implies a change driven by conviction. In my father's case, however, he went from being a Jew who didn't go to synagogue to a Christian who didn't go to church.

By the time the Judaism had cascaded down to my father there was pretty much nothing left of it to apostatize from. The Hanukkah light had gone out in the Friedeberg/Fraser family slowly, over a long period of time. Harold and Baba had had such a chaotic existence – divorcing, changing names and addresses and schools for the children, and then the war – it was hard for a faith of ritual observance to survive all that. Louis would have been horrified that his grandson had converted to Christianity– and his wife, Rose, too, with her memories of the Łódź ghetto. But the more I think about it, the more I understand that it wasn't really my father's doing. For generations, the Friedebergs had been trying to fit in and play along. To be more English than the English. The faith of Moses was abandoned in stages. And at the end of the line was a rather lost priest, a Canon of St Paul's Cathedral, at the heart of the establishment, now sitting at the side of the road by Samuel's Liverpool synagogue.

In the late Middle Ages, Kabbalistic thinkers developed a controversial teaching about reincarnation known as the *gilgul*. The soul is destined for God. But in order to reach God, it has to perform all 613 of the biblical commandments, usually not possible in one lifetime. The soul passes or rolls down the generations – the Hebrew word *gilgul* means 'rolling'– until all the commandments have been fulfilled. It is sometimes argued that Job 1:21 is describing precisely this transmigration of souls: 'Naked I came from my mother's womb, and naked shall I return there.'

The proponents of the eighteenth-century Jewish Enlightenment, the Haskalah, hated all this superstitious mumbo-jumbo, and did all they could to disparage it. But in the popular imagination, and especially within Hasidic thought and folklore, this sort of mystical thinking had considerable explanatory power. The *gilgul* is not a million miles away from the idea of transgenerational haunting as described by Abraham and Torok. There is an irrational element in theology and in the folk literature it inspires – just as in children's fairy tales – that encourages our repressed inner fears to come to the surface. Such literature can offer us representations of a sort of psychic leakage that mirror back to ourselves so much that we deny in the name of a more cautious and structured rationality. Freud himself may have been profoundly influenced by the Haskalah, but his suggestion that the unconscious expresses itself in dreams is an extension of a much more Hasidic sensibility. This is partly why I take theological mumbo-jumbo seriously.

It was a century ago, in 1914, that the Russian socialist and ethnographer Shlomo Ansky first published his curious

Yiddish play, *A Dybbuk, or Between Two Worlds*. On the surface it's a Jewish ghost story and a sideways development of the whole *gilgul* theme. The story is roughly this. Hannan is a penniless yeshiva student. Leah is the beautiful daughter of a greedy father. But theirs was a love that was not to be. Hannan is considered too poor by Leah's father, so he arranges her engagement to another man. When Hannan finds out, the young theologian rejects God, embraces the devil and falls dead with grief.

The next day, prepared in her bridal gown for a man she doesn't want to marry, and with guests already beginning to assemble, a desperate Leah runs out to the cemetery. Driven mad with distress, she collapses in front of Hannan's grave and embraces it, beyond care that she is meddling in something far beyond her understanding. She begs and begs. He must rise from the dead and enter into her body. He must make his home in her. Her soul would be big enough to carry both of them. So Hannan is resurrected as a spiritual half-life, a dybbuk, and rises to take possession of her body. The local rabbi is summoned to exorcize the dybbuk from Leah. When he succeeds, she is faced with a choice – to carry on and marry a rich man she does not love, or to be reunited with Hannan in death. The curtain closes.

The play's subtitle, 'Between Two Worlds', is superficially a reference to the spiritual liminality of the dybbuk, suspended between life and death, fully inhabiting neither. But it's more than that. Ansky was a curious figure. Both intensely secular – a left-wing political radical who had given up on the ritual side of Jewish life – and also strangely religious in a cultural way, both Russian and Jewish, as he struggled with the extent to which assimilation among the Enlightenment intelligentsia meant a betrayal of his peasant roots. 'Possessing an eternal longing for Jewishness,' he recounted at a literary banquet held in his honour in 1910, 'I nevertheless threw myself in all directions and left to work for other people. My life was broken, split, torn.'

In response to this longing, throughout the period 1911–15, Ansky led several ethnographical expeditions to many dozens of East European shtetls throughout the Pale of Settlement – a strip of land roughly 500 kilometres wide, stretching from the Black Sea to the Baltic. Created by Catherine the Great in 1791, after several failed attempts to remove the Jews from Russia permanently, the Pale was an area in which most Russian Jews were confined. At the turn of the nineteenth century, it contained 40 per cent of the world's Jews.

Ansky is partly responsible for the whole *Fiddler on the Roof* romanticization of the Pale of Settlement. Anticipating some further catastrophe, rightly as it turned out, and trying to reconnect with his own sense of being Jewish, he went out to gather everything he could find: old prayers, stories, mythologies, jewellery, antiques, manuscripts, photographs of provincial synagogues. On 1 January 1915, he wrote desperately to the Warsaw Yiddish daily newspaper entreating his fellow Jews to do the same: 'Record, take it down, and collect. See to it that nothing is lost or forgotten . . . record everything, knowing thereby that you are collecting necessary material for the construction of Jewish history during this horribly important and terribly vital moment. . . . Whatever can be recorded should be recorded and whatever can be photographed should be photographed.'

Why did all of this painstaking research result in a ghost story? Caught between powerful and competing polarities, stuck in some curious in-between place, Ansky's own existence had become a kind of ghostly half-life – neither one thing or another. Ansky was himself the dybbuk.

In 1915, the year after Ansky published *The Dybbuk*, his contemporary Sigmund Freud, also of course a secularized Jew, began to draft one of his seminal works, *Mourning and Melancholia*. Though very different in form, Freud's work is essentially about the same thing and driven by the same instinct. In mourning, Freud argues, one is grieving for the loss of something concrete. And because this loss is the loss of something specific and tangible, the process of mourning can be worked through in the conscious mind. The function of mourning, he says, 'is to detach the survivor's memories and hopes from the dead'. In time, the energy of grief is worked through and is drained of much of its intensity. Melancholia, by contrast, is an unconscious grief for something intangible, something that cannot be named and that one doesn't even know has been lost. Because the object of the loss cannot be named, the loss cannot be processed by the conscious mind. As the loss is not directed towards the absence of anything out there in the world – at least, it is not recognized as such – the pain of loss is internalized. In mourning, the loss is the loss of something out there. In melancholia, the loss is of something inside, a loss of self. In this way, Freud says, melancholia is often linked to suicide. Because the pain of loss cannot be named, it eats away at the self, unrecognized.

One of the principal strategies of psychoanalysis is the conversion of unconscious pain into conscious pain, the changing of self-directed melancholia into plain mourning. Or to put it another way, psychoanalysis is the summoning up of ghosts from out of the shadows. Only thus can they be exorcized. Psychoanalysis is an Enlightenment variation on the Jewish ghost story.

4. Romans

The dybbuk is neither one thing nor another – neither alive nor dead. Its very existence is a transgression of some ultimate boundary. Other fantastical figures have this same boundary-crossing quality too. In Greek mythology, the chimera is a fire-breathing monster with the head of a lion, the body of a goat and the tail of a snake. Another derivative meaning of 'chimera' is something that is hoped for but is impossible to achieve.

The following chapters of this book are ostensibly all about theology and specifically about the formation of the boundary between Jew and Christian; what these boundaries are defending and whose interests they serve. At the same time, these chapters, although informed by contemporary scholarship, are just as personal as the more obviously revealing parts of this memoir. What is going on here is not the theology of the academy, but theology in the service of self-understanding. The boundaries I am interested in here are the ones that turn me into some sort of chimera – a strange, seemingly impossible combination of theological allegiances, in which my own integration as a person is longed for yet permanently unattainable.

I.

In the early hours of 12 June 1994, Rabbi Menachem Mendel Schneerson – widely known as the Rebbe – passed away at the Mount Sinai Beth Israel medical centre in New York at the age of ninety-four. He had been ill for some time after a stroke that left the right side of his body completely paralysed and in the three months immediately prior to his death he had fallen into a coma. But despite his considerable age and several infirmities there were many within the world-wide Hasidic community known as Chabad-Lubavitch who were not expecting him to die at all. They said he was the Messiah, the man who was going to gather together the people of Israel, rebuild the temple and reign as God's king on earth. Such a man could never die.

Messiah means 'anointed one' – anointing being the manner in which the ancient kings of Israel were marked out as royal and bearing divine approval. Both political and religious, the Messiah was a figure of legend, a human leader who would return the fortunes of the people of Israel to the golden era of David and Solomon. According to the prophet Isaiah, one of the most enthusiastic proponents of messianic expectation, the Messiah would be so powerful that he would destroy hunger and illness, even death itself.

Even today there are many who do not believe that the Rebbe has actually died. Long after his funeral, at the Chabad-Lubavitch yeshiva on Eastern Parkway in Crown Heights, Brooklyn, New York – the global headquarters of the Rebbe's operation – they still fly white flags each marked with a golden crown and a single word below it: 'Moshiach'. A banner across the front door of the yeshiva proclaims, 'Messiah is here,' next to the image of Schneerson. Throughout Israel, at the side of the road and posted on buildings and the back of traffic signs, from Jerusalem to Tel Aviv and beyond, many thousands of images of the kindly face of the Rebbe, with silver beard and fedora hat, look out over the street, complete with Hebrew text declaring his continued monarchy. The

Rebbe never actually visited Israel, but his face is still everywhere. When Chabad Jews gather together in packed halls or synagogues, they will bounce up and down with massive enthusiasm and huge collective energy, and sing out confidently: 'Long live our Master, Teacher, and Rabbi. King Messiah, for ever and ever.'

The modern revival of messianic expectation within Judaism began with the advent of Hasidism in the eighteenth century and, in particular, with the mystical theology of Rabbi Israel ben Eliezer, better known as the Baal Shem Tov, from what is now northern Ukraine. Not unlike Methodism in Christianity – the Baal Shem Tov and John Wesley were almost exact contemporaries – Hasidism was a movement of populist piety and a reaction against the elite and dry intellectualism of the Jewish Enlightenment, the Haskalah. Joyous and emotional, raucous even, Hasidism emphasizes a religion of the heart and encourages crescendos of popular sentiment, often expressed as messianic enthusiasm. As the Rebbe himself often pointed out, messianism was not itself new or limited to the Hasidim. From Rashi to Nachmanides, even the Gaon of Vilnius – who was otherwise deeply hostile to the boisterous Hasidic enterprise – most of the famous rabbinic thinkers of the past had contributed in some way to messianic expectation. Even so mainstream a figure as Maimonides had messianism as one of his basic principles of Judaism: 'I believe with full faith in the coming of the Messiah. And even though he tarries, with all that, I await his arrival with every day.'

Within the Chabad community, however, and throughout the Rebbe's period in office, the expectation had been growing that the Messiah was now close at hand. He had tarried long enough. 'We are now very near the approaching footsteps of the Messiah,' Schneerson proclaimed during his opening address as leader in January 1951. His predecessor had prophesied that the messianic age would begin with the seventh Chabad Rebbe. And Menachem Mendel Schneerson was the seventh.

As the Rebbe approached old age, he began to preach more and more about the need for a crescendo of piety so as to trigger the arrival of the Messiah. Throughout his period in office this warm and charismatic man had taken a movement that had nearly been wiped out by the Holocaust and massively grown its following through an emphasis on missionary activity among his fellow Jews. But what was to happen next? 'Is it possible that the Lubavitchers feel that they do not need to worry about a successor because the Rebbe himself will be the Savior?' asked *The New York Times* in 1985, picking up on the growing sense of anticipation within Chabad-Lubavitcher circles.

The Rebbe was careful not to describe himself directly as the Messiah, and he sought to dissuade others from doing so when he heard them pronounce him thus. He was nonetheless instrumental in stimulating messianic arousal among his followers. In 1990, Saddam Hussein invaded Kuwait and threatened to burn half of Israel to the ground. In January 1991, the First Gulf War began and the Coalition forces quickly destroyed much of Hussain's army, driving them out of Kuwait. Among the Hasidim, the success of the war and the deliverance of Israel from danger were taken as miraculous signs that the *ketz* (the time of the messianic arrival) was close at hand. Later that year, the Rebbe preached what became a famous sermon, urging his followers to redouble their efforts to bring about the messianic age. 'How is it that ten Jews can gather together, and notwithstanding everything that has been done, we have not brought Messiah? It's utterly incomprehensible.'

Up to 10,000 people are said to have gathered at the Rebbe's funeral. After it a sense of existential crisis split the movement. Some continued to maintain that he was the Messiah and some stopped believing. As many argued, death was not in the messianic script, so the Rebbe could not have been the Messiah after all. Among those who kept on believing were a number who speculated that the Rebbe had never actually died and others who maintained that although he had died he would one day return from the dead. Others argued that death had liberated him from the physical constraints of earthbound existence. Acrimony inevitably grew between the so-called Meshichistim – those who continued to maintain his messianic status – and the non-Meshichistim, who changed their minds and admitted they had been wrong, or who claimed they had never believed it in the first place.

Yet the Meshichistim continued to maintain their dominance of the Chabad movement. The greatest population of Lubavitchers is now to be found in Israel, with their largest yeshivah in Safed, and they continue to be firmly committed to the Rebbe as being the Messiah. As David Berger, a campaigning opponent of Meshichist theology insists, the messianic strain in Chabad-Lubavitch remains extremely vigorous across Israel:

> In Safed, virtually every student wears a skullcap adorned with the messianist slogan, 'May our Master, Teacher and Rabbi the King Messiah live forever,' which begins with the Hebrew word *yechi*;* in Netanya most do; in Bnei Brak about half do; at a 2010 event in Torat Emet yeshiva in Jerusalem a giant *yechi* poster adorned the wall; *yechi* appears at the top of the home page of the Herzliya and Ramat Aviv yeshivas; the yeshiva of Mitzpeh Yitzhar is clearly messianist.

* *Yechi* is shorthand for the phrase 'Yechi Adoneinu Moreinu v'Rabbinu Melech haMoshiach l'olam vo'ed', which translates as 'Long live our Master, our Teacher, and our Rabbi, King Messiah, for ever and ever.'

Yet, despite their differences, neither side completely broke contact with the other. They have separate synagogue newsletters and they celebrate the day of the Rebbe's death differently, but they are bonded together by family ties and a shared history – and they both continue to await the day of redemption, whether under the Rebbe's kingship or someone else's. But whatever the nature of their continued disagreement, and however intense it is, no one from within the Lubavitcher community, or indeed from the wider Jewish community as a whole, has claimed that the other side are not really Jews. That's just not a question, not even for their sternest critics, like David Berger. Of course the Meshichistim are Jews. They are just mistaken, say their opponents. Gravely mistaken, argues David Berger, and should be disbarred from high office within the Orthodox community. But being mistaken doesn't stop them from being Jews. The posters of the Rebbe that continue to be put up throughout Israel are not being angrily torn down by protesters who claim that they are propaganda from some proselytizing non-Jewish sect. No, those who proclaim the Rebbe as the Messiah are a part of the rich diversity of Jewish practice: outliers, perhaps; heretics, even – but still clearly Jewish.

All of which raises an important question: why weren't the first followers of Jesus understood in the same way? How come those Jews who originally proclaimed Jesus as the Messiah are not understood as fellow Jews, albeit heretical ones?

2.

Imagine for a moment that a committed member of the Meshichistim community decides to make a film about the Rebbe. 'The King is Alive,' they call it. As a Chabad-Lubavitch production, it is a film with a clear evangelistic intent towards fellow Jews. The film is in Yiddish, made for a Yiddish-speaking audience. The Rebbe is the Messiah, the film powerfully proclaims. He lives. And to everyone's surprise, the film becomes something of a hit, widely shared on the Internet.

But it is not just fellow Jews that are arrested by the film's powerful message. Given English subtitles, 'The King is Alive' begins to attract a modest but committed international audience. Small groups of non-Jews begin to meet in backrooms to discuss the film and to explain to each other how much the Rebbe's teaching affected them, how it made a difference in their lives. These meetings often end with a moment of prayer. Let us say these groups call themselves the Fellowship of the Rainbow.

The name is chosen for a reason. In Genesis, chapter 9, following the story of the great flood, God makes a deal with Noah and his children. Never again will the earth be flooded, God promises. God and Noah agree a deal between themselves that humanity will keep certain laws – the Seven Noahide Laws – and that, in turn, God will guarantee human flourishing. The sign for this agreement, this so-called covenant, will be the rainbow. The important thing to underline here is that God makes a pact with humanity in general, and not just with Jews.

Later, in Genesis, chapter 17, God makes a covenant exclusively with the Jewish people, the Bnei Abraham, and makes circumcision the special sign for this covenant. But in Genesis 9 the covenant is made with all the people of the earth, the Bnei Noah. So calling themselves the Rainbow Fellowship was clearly a making a statement.

Back in 1983 (and this bit is true), the Rebbe began a

campaign to inform Gentiles of the importance of the Noahide laws and he encouraged the Chabad into a form of missionary activity with the Gentiles, focusing on this specific aspect of Jewish theology. The Rebbe even persuaded President Ronald Reagan, himself a committed Christian, to join in his campaign to promote the Noahide laws. In 1982, Ronald Reagan issued the following extraordinary proclamation.

National Day of Reflection
By the President of the United States of America
A Proclamation

Amid the distractions and concerns of our daily existence, it is appropriate that Americans pause to reflect on the ancient ethical principles and moral values which are the foundation of our character as a nation. We seek, and steadfastly pursue, the benefits of education. But education must be more than factual enlightenment – it must enrich the character as well as the mind. One shining example for people of all faiths of what education ought to be is that provided by the Lubavitch movement, headed by Rabbi Menachem Schneerson, a worldwide spiritual leader who will celebrate his 80th birthday on April 4, 1982. The Lubavitcher Rebbe's work stands as a reminder that knowledge is an unworthy goal unless it is accompanied by moral and spiritual wisdom and understanding. He has provided a vivid example of the eternal validity of the Seven Noahide Laws, a moral code for all of us regardless of religious faith. May he go from strength to strength. In recognition of the Lubavitcher Rebbe's 80th birthday, the Senate and the House of Representatives of the United States in Congress assembled have issued House Joint Resolution 447 to set aside April 4, 1982, as a 'National Day of Reflection.'

NOW, THEREFORE, I, RONALD REAGAN, President of the United States of America, do hereby proclaim April 4, 1982, as National Day of Reflection. IN WITNESS WHEREOF, I have hereunto set my hand this 3rd day of April, in the year of our Lord nineteen hundred and eighty-two, and of the Independence of the United States of America the two hundred and sixth.

Ronald Reagan

Returning to my thought experiment: the Rainbow Fellowship of Gentiles and Jews had some plausible claim to be internationally recognized followers of the Rebbe, however contested that claim may be by the non-Meshichistim. But what did other Jews make of this Rainbow Fellowship? For the most part they are ignored by the wider Jewish community or dismissed as a peculiar idiosyncrasy. Gentile Jew is an oxymoron, almost an insult.

But for the Meshichistim themselves, the Rainbow Fellowship poses quite a conundrum. After all, it was the Rebbe himself who had tried to recruit Gentiles to follow the Noahide Laws. And now that they had become enthusiastic about the Rebbe and convinced by his messianic claims, perhaps there was a place for them. Even the Meshichistim disagree among themselves about this. Most insist that all of the Rebbe's followers must convert to Judaism and follow all of the Jewish law. Others think that there might conceivably be a special status for the Rainbow Fellowship as those who acknowledge the Rebbe as the Messiah. They may not be Jews, but they are certainly fellow travellers. Some Meschichistim think that the Rainbow Fellowship should become full Jews and get themselves circumcised before they can be acknowledged as full members of the Rebbe-following religion, as it were. Others think being Bnei Noah is enough, and that it gives them more than observer status. The more conservative majority look down on the Rainbow Fellowship. But a few radical voices think they are the future.

This is where my fictional account of the foundation of a new religion called Rainbowism takes a fantastical turn. Imagine some massive catastrophe strikes the Jewish people. Perhaps Iran drops a nuclear bomb on Jerusalem. Or the Syrians successfully invade Israel. Imagine the Jewish people come to be persecuted by some new world power. Perhaps none of these scenarios is as fantastical as it should be. Anyway, imagine some great crisis. In such a world the Meschichistim, persecuted as Jews, struggle to survive. Shunned by the mainstream Jewish community, but violently persecuted as Jews by the new world power, they dwindle and eventually perish. The Gentile Rainbow Fellowship, however – because they are not ethnically Jews – are not persecuted in this new world order. Indeed, they come to flourish.

Those mainstream Jews who didn't much care for the Meshichistim or their claims about the Rebbe's messianic status adopt an 'I told you so' attitude towards the growing Rainbow Fellowship. The flourishing of non-Jews who had appropriated Jewish theology serves only to underline how right they were to be suspicious of the messianic claims made by the Rebbe and on his behalf. Meshichistim theology was never proper Judaism, they say. And here is the proof. David Berger had warned of the 'scandal of orthodox indifference' to the messianic claims made by some in the Chabad-Lubavitch community. The remnants of the Meshichistim realize too late what it meant to allow the Rainbow Fellowship to count themselves as fellow Schneerson followers. The Bnei Noah had become a cuckoo in the nest.

Fast forward a few centuries and Menachem Mendel Schneerson has been stripped of his Judaism. He is depicted as a blond-haired and blue-eyed saviour. His Jewishness is barely mentioned. Instead, he is remembered most of all as the founder of Rainbowism, a universalist religion of the Bnei Noah. Rainbowism even openly derides 'the Jews' for their narrowness and exclusivism – as well as for rejecting the Messiah. The Jewish Meshichistim, the original followers of the Rebbe, those who first proclaimed him as the Messiah, have been written out of the story.

I have made all this up, of course – but to illustrate a point. What I am proposing in this chapter is that this is, broadly speaking, how Christianity came to be formed in the first few centuries after the death of the man called Jesus, who was proclaimed the Messiah by a number of Jews after his death. Jesus-following Jews, those who were to Jesus what the Meshichistim are to Schneerson, end up being squeezed out of history by the developing idea of orthodoxy, both Jewish and Christian. In the first four centuries after the death of Jesus the Messiah, Christians began to jettison the Jewishness of Jesus, reimagining him as a citizen of nowhere. Taken up by the Roman Empire, still at war with the Jews, the Jesus of memory is divested of his Jewishness. And pressed from the other side, in reaction to the catastrophe of the destruction of the Temple, and threatened by Christian evangelism, Jews seek to define their own religious identity more strictly, by also rejecting the Jewishness of Jesus. By the fourth century, Jesus-following Jews are a rarity, persecuted from both sides. The development of an official version of religion, called orthodoxy, develops in parallel among Jews and Christians, both defining themselves in opposition to the other, both thinking it important to define their boundaries in such a way that Jewish Jesus followers, the Jewish Meshichistim, are excluded. Like my fiction of the Bnei Noah – but this time not a fiction – this is the story of how Jesus lost his Jewishness.

3

Jesus wasn't a Christian. He wasn't the first Christian. He wasn't even a Christian with an interesting Jewish backstory. Nowhere does this charismatic carpenter from Galilee suggest that he wants to start a new religion. On the contrary: 'I was sent only to the lost sheep of the house of Israel,' he tells a woman in Matthew's Gospel.

Yes, Jesus would constantly argue with the religious authorities of his day. But arguing with religious authority has always been a longstanding Jewish tradition. Jesus was Jewish, completely Jewish – he had a Jewish mother, he was circumcised according to the law, he kept kosher, his Bible was the Bible of Abraham, Isaac and Jacob, he attended his local Galilee synagogue, he taught in the Temple throughout his life and he made pilgrimage to the Temple for the special feasts. And he died Jewish, mocked as the King of the Jews. According to the Book of Acts, the followers of Jesus first got to be called Christians in Antioch decades after Jesus himself had been killed. Christianity is unique among the world's religious traditions in so far as its founder was not himself a member of the religion that he had inadvertently founded.

Jesus' first followers were Jewish agricultural labourers and fishermen. They were the first-century equivalent of the Meshichistim. Yes, they adopted a distinctive form of Judaism, drawing more from the prophets and the eschatological literature of the Hebrew Scriptures. They were more concerned with the spirit than the letter of the law and increasingly hostile to what they saw as the abuses of the Temple in Jerusalem. But in all of this they were well within the bandwidth of recognizably Jewish practice. After all, criticizing the abuses of the Temple's priestly caste, and how the Temple sacrifices were being performed, was a subject of almost continual interest to the writers of the Hebrew Scriptures. Jesus' polemic against the Temple was not that of a hostile outsider – indeed, he called the Temple 'my Father's house' at the very same time as he was attacking the money-changers. He was simply channelling the spirit of Jeremiah, Amos, the Psalmist and others. Jesus attacked the management of the Temple in a way that only a Jew could have done.

First-century Judaism was a patchwork of different and disagreeing theological traditions – the traditionalist Pharisees, the aristocratic Sadducees, the separatist Essenes, the politically minded Zealots, free-wheeling prophets like John the Baptist, followers of the 'fourth philosophy', Nazarites and various types of sages. The Talmud claims there were some seventy different traditions of being Jewish. The original followers of Jesus were certainly no more divergent from the Jewish theological mainstream than, say, the Essenes, who took themselves off to the caves above the Dead Sea and followed their own charismatic leader, the so-called Teacher of Righteousness. Indeed, the idea that during the first century there was even such a thing as a Jewish theological mainstream is actually highly implausible. Judaism was yet to be centralized around a set of agreed practices. The boundary lines that we have come to be familiar with that separate one 'religion' from another were yet to be established.

In other words, the very first Christians weren't Christians at all. They were Jews – Bnei Abraham – and they kept the Torah. 'Do not think that I have come to abolish the law or the prophets,' Jesus says in Matthew's Gospel. 'I have not come to abolish but to fulfil. For truly, I tell you, until heaven and earth pass away, not one letter, not one stroke of a letter, will pass from the law until all is accomplished. Therefore, whoever breaks one of the least of these commandments, and teaches others to do the same, will be called least in the kingdom of heaven.' Clearly, this is not a religion for the Bnei Noah; it is for the Bnei Abraham. Read literally, this passage from Matthew implies that Christians are also obliged to keep kosher and Shabbat. It is commonly assumed that the Old Testament is the Jewish part of the Bible and the New Testament is the Christian part. But that is a huge misunderstanding. The Old and the New Testaments are both thoroughly and indivisibly Jewish.

Among the many reasons to bear this in mind is that it provides important context for the apparently anti-Jewish and anti-Pharisee polemic that seems to exist throughout some of the Gospel accounts. Jesus may call the Pharisees a 'brood of vipers' and 'children of the devil' – but these were not originally insults being flung against Jews by non-Jews, as they later became. These and other passages have often been deemed the source code of Christian antisemitism. And they were certainly extensively exploited by later Christians as justification for centuries of anti-Jewish hatred. But reminding oneself that these arguments, however heated, were originally arguments between Jews, not against Jews, shows how peculiar it became to use them as the basis of antisemitism. Antisemitism is not just the greatest sin of the institutional Church – and there are lots to choose from. It is also its greatest mistake. It is only when Christians begin to regard themselves as some sort of separate group, independent of Judaism (like my fictional Fellowship of the Rainbow), that these passages start to be misread as being about 'them' rather than the wider 'us'.

4

But not all of Jesus' original followers were Jewish. Some of those who heard him preach and were inspired by his message were Gentiles. The Roman Empire was a pretty cosmopolitan place. Jews themselves lived throughout the empire. From the beginning of the third century BC, the Hebrew Scriptures had been translated into Greek to cater for those Jews who were primarily (or even exclusively) Greek-speaking. Most of the Jews who had been exiled in Babylon did not return home, after having established thriving communities in the cities of Mesopotamia. There were substantial Jewish communities in Rome and in Egypt and in the area we now call Turkey. Jews had spread and flourished throughout the empire, and Gentiles in turn had settled in the major population centres of Judaea.

Even conversion to Judaism was broadly accepted, with different schools of thought differing only over the level of strictness for admission – but not the basic principle. In keeping with their overall philosophy, the House of Hillel took a generally liberal line, the House of Shammai a more conservative one. The House of Hillel famously deemed as acceptable for conversion a candidate who mocked his teacher by asking for the whole of the Torah to be explained to him quickly, 'whilst standing on one foot'. In other words, even those who convert with scant knowledge of the law can be accepted as converts. Shammai, on the other hand, disapproved of those who presented themselves for conversion without the proper seriousness. These two schools of thought thus disagreed about the manner of conversion, but they both agreed on the basic principle of the acceptability of conversion to Judaism. So there was nothing especially unusual about the fact that Jesus had Gentile followers.

The question that much exercised the first communities of Jesus' followers was precisely how these new Gentiles ought to be included as members of the same religious community as those who understood themselves as Jews. Obviously all Jewish Jesus-followers were obliged to keep the Torah and go to the Temple for the special feasts. There wasn't even a question about that: they were Jews, after all. But what was required of Gentile Jesus-followers? And specifically, were they expected to be circumcised? It was the standard Jewish practice to circumcise male converts immediately on conversion, whatever their age.

The New Testament Book of Acts lays out this conundrum. For example, it tells the story of a suspicious delegation from the Jewish Jerusalem church travelling up to visit a new Gentile church that had been established at Antioch. The conservative-minded delegation of Jerusalem Jews made it pretty clear to these new Gentile Christians of Antioch that they were required to go and get themselves circumcised in order for them to become full and proper followers of Jesus. The Antioch Christians were not entirely happy about this and refused. They wanted the Jesus bit without all of the being-Jewish bit. And this sparked the first great argument within the church, at a gathering known as the Jerusalem Conference, sometime around 50 AD, and some twenty or so years after the death of Jesus.

What was at stake here was whether the Jesus movement was predominantly Jewish, with a few, rather curious outliers – Gentiles who had converted to a very particular form of Judaism – or whether it was something that extended beyond the religion of the Jewish people and reached out to all humanity. Those who argued for this latter position were not necessarily religious innovators. After all, they could use the Hebrew Scriptures themselves as justification for their position. Hadn't Isaiah given a pretty heavy hint that one day the religion of the Jews would be opened out to include all people, even the goyim?

> And foreigners who join themselves to the Lord,
>> to minister to him, to love the name of the Lord,
>> and to be his servants,
> all who keep the Sabbath, and do not profane it,
>> and who hold fast my covenant—
> these I will bring to my holy mountain,
>> and make them joyful in my house of prayer;
> their burnt offerings and their sacrifices
>> will be accepted on my altar;
> for my house shall be called a house of prayer
>> for all peoples.
> Thus says the Lord God,
>> who gathers the outcasts of Israel,
> I will gather others to them
>> besides those already gathered.
>
> (Isaiah 56:6–8)

Isaiah was Jesus' favourite book of the Bible – certainly the one he quotes from the most. Arguably, the ideology of the so-called New Testament begins with Isaiah. So, Jesus-following Jews might have every reason to expect that the God of Israel would reach out beyond the people of Israel to the world beyond. There was certainly a theological case for the inclusion of Jesus-following Gentiles into the broader arena of Temple Judaism, which was already a pretty inclusive gathering. With Isaiah, globalization had its first champion.

It was St Paul, however, who first took this emphasis on the universal relevance of the God spoken about by Jesus, and turned it into a central feature of what we now call Christianity. Paul was a Jew himself (indeed, a Pharisee by training), but also a Roman citizen born into the Jewish diaspora in modern-day Turkey, and thus the nearest thing to a citizen of the world that a Jew could be. For Paul, the God that he recognized in Jesus was absolutely the God that was promised to Jews in the Hebrew Scriptures, but – and this was his world-changing idea – He was also a God that was promised to all humanity.

It now seems obvious to Christians that the God spoken about by Jesus is a God that seeks out the salvation of all people, irrespective of race, nationality or culture. But it wasn't at all obvious to many of Paul's contemporaries, and it took some arguing on his part. In Christ there is neither Jew nor Greek, Paul insisted. You don't need to be ethnically Jewish to be saved. With Jesus, the special deal that God had made with the Jewish people, the Abrahamic covenant, had been extended to include all non-Jews as well. It wasn't that Paul denied the idea that God had established a special relationship with the Jewish people in the first place. All those who are 'in Christ' are 'Abraham's offspring', he maintained. Yes, the Jews were the chosen people – but now, Paul declared, being chosen was open to all.

On the question of circumcision, Paul was absolutely clear: Gentiles were not required to get themselves circumcised. Jesus-followers who were Jews followed the Jewish law, like Jesus himself. So of course they were obliged to be circumcised – as Jesus himself was. But Gentile Jesus-followers, on the other hand, were not required to follow the specifics of the Jewish law because, obviously, they were not Jews. As with Roman citizenship, being a 'Christian' did not require any particular ethnicity and was compatible with a variety of different cultural practices.

But many in the Jerusalem Church, under the leadership of Jesus' brother James were not persuaded by what they took to be Paul's theological innovation. Acts 15.5 describes their opposition:

> Then some of the believers who belonged to the party of the Pharisees stood up and said, 'The Gentiles must be circumcised and required to keep the law of Moses.'

This is a fascinating passage, for it creates an impression of the first church of (what would become) Christianity that is wholly unlike anything most Christians today would be able to imagine. The very idea that the Jerusalem Church of Jesus-followers included those 'who belonged to the party of the Pharisees' and that they were arguing with Paul, himself Pharisee and a one-time student of the great Pharisaic teacher Gamaliel, comes as quite a challenge to those who imagine the early Church to be, as it were, 'Christian'. No, this meeting was essentially a Pharisaic dispute, an argument between various temple-going Jews about the meaning of God's relationship with His people. It could hardly have been a more quintessentially Jewish scene. Yet this was what the early Church looked like.

But what this argument was absolutely not about – though it soon came to be seen this way – was the significance of the law per se. This is important to emphasize because for a long time one very common interpretation of Paul's disagreement with historic Judaism was that he attacked Judaism for being a religion of legalistic box-ticking. This interpretation was especially prominent among later Protestant Reformers who argued that the Old Testament erroneously teaches that we are saved by following the law and accruing merit points, whereas the New Testament teaches that we are saved through faith alone. This law/faith contrast has been used to establish a fundamental difference of theology over which Christianity and Judaism apparently disagree, and one that, as some Christians would have it, demonstrates the obvious superiority of the Christian world view.

One of the most important developments in biblical studies during the latter half of the twentieth century is the so-called 'New Perspective on Paul'. This demonstrated convincingly that the law/faith distinction was an act of reading back into the Bible the categories of much later debates, like those between Augustine and Pelagius and, even more so, between Luther and the Roman Catholic Church. Following the ground-breaking work of E. P. Sanders in his *Paul and Palestinian Judaism* (1977), it began to be increasingly recognized that first-century Jews didn't actually believe that you got to be saved by following the law, but rather by being a part of the people of God. And following the law – for example, on circumcision – was simply the way in which membership of this community was marked out. The New Perspective theologian James Dunn famously called circumcision 'the badge of the covenant' – not a way of getting saved, but a mark that you had been.

So the difference between Paul's theology and that of his Jewish contemporaries was not that he rejected Judaism as being what the Protestant reformers would later disparagingly refer to as 'works-righteousness' – a phrase that carries something of the same negative connotation as 'box-ticking'. Rather, Paul simply believed the set of God's people had been expanded to include non-Jews. This may seem a technical point, but it is important because the over-extension of the law/faith distinction has been extensively used to paint a picture of Judaism as a going-through-the-motions type of religion, rather than a matter-of-really-meaning-it religion (Christianity). This readily fed into a disparagement of Judaism and its theology, as fundamentally insincere, and led to the trope of the shifty, hypocritical Jew. With the law/faith distinction and the description of the New Testament as new – thus replacing the old – the anti-Judaism of later centuries is read back into the Bible. But Paul didn't disparage the Jewish theology of the covenant between God and his people in the slightest – he merely wanted to extend it: salvation was no longer to be an ethnic privilege. For Paul, the Gospel message was an expansion of the old, and certainly not any sort of replacement for it.

Looking forward, however, it is probably the case that Paul's argument for the inclusion of non-Jews into the fellowship of Jesus-followers turned out to be the first move in the separation of Judaism and what later came to be called Christianity. But that is not how it would have been experienced at the time. Winning the argument that Gentile Christians didn't need to keep the whole Jewish law to be Jesus-followers didn't yet mean the Church instantly became an international body. It was simply that the Jerusalem Church had been forced to accept that it had a legitimate overseas mission that did not abide by the same rules of traditional Jewish practice. Even so, from this point onwards there were two types of 'Christians' – Jewish Christians who were Jews, and some pretty conservative Jews at that; and Gentile Christians, who were largely exempt from the requirements of most of the law, including circumcision.

ſ.

What turned this two-track arrangement world-historically toxic was an event that is remembered by Jews to this day as a turning point in the fortunes of the Jewish people: the war between the Jews and the Romans, a war that included the destruction of the Temple and the expulsion of Jews from Jerusalem.

Because Jewish Jesus-followers were still Jews, the Roman war against the Jews was as much a war against them as it was against those Jews who did not recognize Jesus as the Jewish Messiah. Details of the subtle differences between the various Jewish sects would have been lost on the Romans. And so it was that the two groups of Jesus-followers increasingly found themselves on opposite sides of a wider political conflict between the Romans and the Jews. This was a defining moment. For this was a conflict during which Gentile Jesus-followers – increasingly called Christians – eventually came to flourish with the conversion to Christianity of the Emperor Constantine, and one in which Jewish Jesus-followers would be effectively banished to the sidelines and written out of history.

In AD 66, after several years of regional government by corrupt Roman occupiers, Jewish resistance to Roman rule began to escalate and a full-scale rebellion broke out. For several decades there had been a period of relative calm between Jews and Romans, but there was always an underlying tension between the occupiers and the occupied. Generally pretty ecumenically minded when it came to the belief systems of others, the Romans were nonetheless particularly wary of the capacity of the Jewish religion to translate itself into political opposition to their rule. Jews, for their part, were highly scornful of the tendency of Romans to 'divinize' a number of their more popular political leaders – Julius Caesar, Augustus, Claudius, Vespasian – after their deaths. By contrast, strict monotheism – 'Hear, O Israel, the Lord is God, the Lord is one' (Deuteronomy 6:4) – is at the very heart of Jewish self-understanding. This difference always had the makings of trouble.

The first-century Jewish writer and historian Josephus recounts the story of an attempt by Herod the Great, the Roman puppet king of Judaea, to erect a golden eagle, a symbol of Roman imperial power, over the gate of the Jerusalem Temple. This was a clear violation of the Jewish law concerning idolatry and thus a blatant insult to the sensibilities of Jewish temple worship. A group of young men climbed up on the Temple ramparts and started hacking at the eagle with axes. The Romans arrested them and burned them alive. Incidents like this kept the Romans alert to the potential of religious commitment to inspire insurrection against their rule – and, of course, Jesus himself was executed on precisely this charge.

In AD 66 a large-scale revolt erupted. Jerusalem Jews attacked and killed several thousand Roman troops, declaring themselves to be an independent Jewish city and even minting coins declaring year one, year two, etc. to celebrate their victory and freedom. They had re-founded Israel. But their victory was to be short-lived. A leadership battle in Rome saw candidates for the job of emperor brandishing their strong-man credentials, and little was more impressive to a Roman audience than victory on foreign soil. It was thus that Vespasian – as it happens, the successful candidate for emperor – came to lead four legions of the Roman army in laying siege to and eventually completely destroying the city of Jerusalem and its Temple.

This was grandstanding on an epic scale, and Vespasian and his son Titus were both indifferent to the immense suffering that they visited on the city. During the siege, starvation and famine set in. 'Wives would snatch food from husbands, children from fathers and – most pitiable sight of all – mothers from the very mouths of their infants,' explained Josephus. One woman, Mary, daughter of Eleazar, roasted her own son for food, Josephus tells us. And those who tried to escape the city were crucified for all to see: 'the soldiers out of rage and hatred amused themselves by nailing their prisoners in different positions.' When the city finally fell, the remaining inhabitants were slaughtered, the Temple was raized to the ground and its liturgical treasures – including the famous golden menorah and a scroll of the Torah – were taken back to Rome and paraded through the streets as trophies of war. The Titus Arch, on the Via Sacra in Rome, was constructed later in the first century to commemorate the destruction of Jerusalem and became the original model for many triumphal arches that were to follow, including the Arc de Triomphe in Paris. It depicts Roman soldiers triumphantly looting the Temple.

The relationship between the Roman Empire and the Jews that lived under its control would never be the same again. Later, in AD 132, Simon bar Kokhba – also declared the Messiah by some – led another revolt against the Roman occupation and this too was brutally suppressed. From the AD 66 rebellion onwards, the Jews came to be treated as enemies of the Roman state and a special case when it came to their policy of freedom of religion. The Romans were generally pretty tolerant of the freedom of occupied people to worship as they wished, and various different cults prospered under Roman occupation – but that freedom was no longer extended to Jews whose Temple was not to be rebuilt. After the suppression of the Bar Kokhba revolt, a new Roman city of Aelia Capitolina was built over the shattered ruins of Jerusalem and Jews were banned from it. From this time on, Jews – including Jesus-following Jews – were the enemies of Rome in a way that non-Jewish Christians were not.

6.

Both Christians and Jews tend to look back on the first few centuries Anno Domini and presume that it was obvious who was Jewish and who Christian. But this is a projection of our current understanding – back then it wasn't at all obvious. Alongside those who were obviously Christian and Jewish other groups existed who were much more difficult to categorize: roughly speaking, Jewish Christians. Of course, they were more like the original Christians, maintaining their Jesus-following in a traditional way. Those in the Church at Jerusalem, with whom Paul had disputed the question of circumcision, were the centre of this Jewish Christianity. And, according to the early Church historian Eusebius, this group fled Jerusalem sometime before the Roman destruction of the Temple, to a place called Pella in what is present-day Jordan.

Little is known about these Jewish Christians after this, though their continued existence can be established mostly through the writings of those who wanted to get rid of them. In the fourth century, historian and theologian Jerome complains in a letter to Augustine:

> There exists a sect among the Jews throughout all the synagogues of the East ... they believe in Christ the Son of God, born of the Virgin Mary; and they say he who suffered under Pontius Pilate and rose again is the same as the one in whom we believe. But while they desire to be both Jews and Christians, they are neither the one nor the other.

Jerome is a representative of what became the official view of the Church, that Christianity and Judaism are mutually exclusive categories. Theology is written by the victors just as much as history. Reconstructing the development of Jewish Christianity through the words of its enemies, it is clear that such a phenomenon survived and flourished enough to worry those who were tasked with clarifying the boundaries of 'legitimate' Christianity.

What is interesting is that it is now almost impossible for us to regard the idea of Jewish Christianity as anything other than some sort of peculiar hybrid of Judaism and Christianity. But the problem with this view is that not only did what we are calling Jewish Christianity actually exist before the formation of Christianity itself, it even preceded the codification of Jewish theology into something we might recognizably now call Judaism. In other words, Jewish Christianity cannot possibly be a hybrid of Christianity and Judaism because it pre-dated both. The fact that we have to strain not to think of it as a hybrid, or that we often use a hyphenated form – Jewish-Christianity – makes it seem obvious that what is going on here is the coming together of two things. That is why it is so hard to conceive of Jewish Christianity as the original expression of Christianity rather than as some peculiar blend. Yet what we call Jewish-Christianity is much closer to the original response by Jews to the teaching of a Jew from Galilee who used the Jewish Scriptures and described himself in that most Jewish of categories, the Messiah.

Nonetheless, during the first few centuries of the Christian era, being 'not Jewish' became a defining feature of Gentile Jesus-following, just as being 'not Christian' became a defining feature of the religion of the early rabbis. The identities of Jews and Christians are constructed on the basis of not being each other. But such is the dominance of the semantic boundaries of what we now call orthodoxy, the religion of Jesus gets hidden in plain sight.

7

The very idea of such a thing as Christian orthodoxy developed in the lead-up to the fourth century and is first stated at the First Council of Nicaea in AD 325, many generations after the death of Jesus. The way Christian history is usually taught, this council was established to settle various long-running disputes about how Jesus could be both human and divine. And it is true that this was partly its purpose. But it was also established to settle the question of who could be a Christian and, in particular, to draw boundaries around Christianity so as to permanently exclude Jesus-following Jews from 'the Church'. The body was set up in order to make religion official and to police the boundaries between who was in and who was out, between Christian and non-Christian.

The important thing about Nicaea was that the meeting was called by the Roman Emperor Constantine. For nearly two centuries, Christian thinkers had been going to great lengths to signal their theological differences from Jews – often with extreme prejudice. Nicaea saw all this become official Church policy. It signalled a decisive moment in the Christian transition from a Jewish movement to an anti-Jewish one, and represents one of the most astonishing U-turns in world history. The Romans killed Jesus, lampooning him as a 'king'. He died on a cross, the Roman's favourite instrument of terror, designed to remind an occupied people of the horrific consequences of resisting Roman rule. Yet less than three centuries later, this cross would be rebranded as a sort of club badge for Christians – not what would happen to you if you resisted the Romans, but rather, precisely what it was to be Roman, the ideological heart of

Roman identity. The Romans not only killed Jesus – but at Nicaea they stole his religion and made it their own.

It was only a couple of decades before Nicaea that the Roman Empire was hunting down Christians, closing down their services and feeding them to lions. On 23 February AD 303, on the orders of the Emperor Diocletian, the church at Nicomedia was torn down, its holy books burnt and its treasures confiscated. The following day, Diocletian issued his first Edict against the Christians, stripping them of legal and property rights, sacking them from official functions, purging them from the army and banning their Scriptures and church assemblies. Christian clergy were forced to make sacrifice to the Roman gods on pain of death. It was the beginning of the so-called Great Persecution, a systematic attempt to eradicate Christianity completely.

The persecution only finally came to an end with the Edict of Milan in AD 313, which established religious toleration for Christians throughout the Roman Empire. By then there was a new emperor in charge, one who was set to transform the fortunes of Christianity from a diminishing and persecuted sect to a globalized world power. The popular story, as told by Eusebius of Caesarea, is that Constantine had a vision of a cross on the eve of the battle of Milvian Bridge in 312, accompanied by the words 'in this sign, conquer'. Because of his vision Constantine ordered his soldiers to mark their shields with the sign of the cross and went on to win a decisive victory that opened up the way to his accession as emperor. It is more likely that, because Constantine had a Christian mother, Helena, he was well disposed towards Christianity from the start.

Much had to change in order for a rag-bag persecuted religion with – in Roman terms – an intellectually dodgy reputation and suspect moral values to turn itself into the official state Church of the Roman Empire. Not least, the Romans had to find a way to downplay all that radical stuff in the teachings of Jesus about the rich and the poor and turning the other cheek. Poverty and forgiveness were not Roman specialities.

The Nicene Creed, still the official summary of the Christian faith and the most important defining document of the Church, describes a religion in which Jesus' radicalism has been expunged. 'For us and for our salvation he came down from heaven, and was incarnate from the Holy Spirit and the Virgin Mary and was made man. For our sake he was crucified under Pontius Pilate; he suffered death and was buried. On the third day he rose again in accordance with the Scriptures.'

What is fascinating about this potted history of Jesus' significance is that it jumps straight from birth to death, ignoring all that happened in between. Nicene Christianity is the religion of Christmas and Easter, the celebration of a man who is either too young or in too much agony to shock us with his radical sermons. The adult Christ who calls his followers to renounce wealth, power and violence is passed over in favour of the gurgling baby and the screaming victim. This sort of religion is much more conducive to the requirements of the Roman Empire – it presents a gagged and glorified saviour who has nothing to say about how we use our money or whether or not we go to war.

Nicene Christianity shifts the focus from what Jesus said to who he was. In making Jesus-following into a cult of the person, downplaying what Jesus taught and preached, the official Church was able to slink away from the more radical demands of the Gospel. And so, in order to emphasize the personality-cult aspect of Jesus-following, under Emperor Constantine the Church began its obsession with architecture. Less than three centuries after Roman masons were chiselling images of the destruction of the Temple on the Titus Arch, they were designing the Church of the Holy Sepulchre in Jerusalem and the Church of the Nativity in Bethlehem. These were huge and expensive imperial projects that took Christian worship out of the house churches and communal halls in which it had been conducted for three centuries and into grand architectural spaces that required state finance to maintain.

Those imperial buildings told the story of the baby and the cross. With their glamour and prestige, they bought off Christian radicalism and sucked the Church into the very ideology of empire that had originally destroyed the person of Jesus. What took place at St Paul's Cathedral during the Occupy movement in 2011 was one tiny consequence of this shift of focus. From Nicaea onwards, Christianity became the creature of empire and the means of its justification. Those who invoked early Christian radicalism – 'What would Jesus do?' said the banners outside St Paul's – did so in opposition to the official Church and its magnificent buildings.

Nicaea also took the Jew out of Jesus. Crucial in this respect was the decision made at Nicaea about the date of Easter. The issue was whether the Last Supper, and thus the whole sequence of events surrounding Easter, should fall at the festival of Passover or not. There was much dispute about this in the first few centuries. For some, as the Scriptures seemed to make pretty clear, Jesus came up to Jerusalem to celebrate the Passover. Thus the Last Supper, even if not strictly a Jewish Passover Seder, was clearly infused with Passover imagery. As such, the Last Supper – that is, the original template for the Eucharist – is a fundamentally Jewish bit of theology. So when Jesus says, 'Do this in remembrance of me,' he is, among other things, commanding a remembrance of the Jewish people being liberated from the land of Egypt. If, however, the date of Easter is to be decoupled from the Passover, then the Jewishness of the Eucharist, and its freedom-celebrating reference to Exodus, is buried – which is precisely what happened at Nicaea. They didn't even provide an alternative way of fixing the date of Easter; they just agreed that Christians mustn't follow the way that Jews calculate the date of Passover. Thus Nicaea severed a fundamental link between Christianity and Judaism. In AD 431 – that is, four centuries after Jesus' death – the Council of Antioch went on to forbid Christians from celebrating Passover with Jews. In other words, the 'this' to which Jesus refers when he said, 'Do this in remembrance of me' – the Passover meal itself – was officially banned by the Church.

8.

The way in which the separation of Christianity and Judaism has been described historically – the story we tell ourselves of their divorce – reflects much about the theological assumptions of the day. Indeed, divorce feels like an easy metaphor to reach for. These two parties, once so close as to be almost indistinguishable, turned against each other painfully and acrimoniously and came to live semi-separate lives, the separation disrupted only by intense periods of persecution – by Christians against Jews.

This divorce model was itself an advance on the nineteenth-century parent-and-child model. In this previous model, Christianity is the child of Judaism and therefore its successor. This model survives in so-called supersessionist accounts in which an old and tired Judaism gives way to the new and vigorous Christianity, as a parent does to its child. These days such accounts survive especially in the minds of right-wing American evangelicals. Judaism is to be esteemed as a parent figure, yes, but they believe the Old Testament has been replaced by Christianity, the New Testament. And thus, although Judaism is respected, there is no longer any need for it. Jews need to be converted to Christianity in order for God's plan to come to fruition.

The exact moment of divorce has been the subject of considerable debate. When I was a student the standard academic consensus was that the Council of Yavneh, apparently around AD 90, was the point at which Christians and Jews went their separate ways. The story told about Yavneh was that after the destruction of the Temple, Judaism needed to re-establish itself. After such an existential catastrophe, the rabbis – who inherited the leadership of 'Judaism' from the Temple priests – required something like a written constitution, a defining of boundaries, a codification of what had previously circulated as oral law. 'Putting a fence around the Torah,' they called it. The Temple had accepted all sorts of Jews through their ethnicity and their participation in its feasts and practices. And that included Jesus-followers. The Temple allowed an inclusive and fuzzy-edged Judaism to flourish, but without it there was nothing to hold all the diverse expressions of Judaism together and so a stricter demarcation of boundaries was required. At Yavneh, the rabbis introduced a prayer into the newly forming post-Temple liturgy, the Birkath ha-Minim – and this included a curse on what they called Nazarenes, that is Jewish Christians. In this way, so the story goes, the Jews kicked the Christians out of the synagogues. And the anger of early Christians towards Jews began from there.

There are various problems with this account, however. First, evidence for the very existence of the Council of Yavneh is hard to come by and frequently disputed. The only written account is from the Babylonian Talmud, and several Jewish scholars now suspect that this may have been a backward interpolation, inventing a very un-Jewish-sounding committee of authority that looks to be modelled on the later councils of the Christian Church – a sort of Jewish Nicaea. Indeed, given the rich diversity of first-century Judaism and the countless theological disagreements among Jews, and given that this was only twenty years after the devastation of the Temple's destruction, how could the rabbis have become so quickly the recognized singular authority on what counts as 'orthodox' Judaism? It is generally understood that it wasn't until the sixth century AD that rabbinic Judaism became the widely accepted official version of Judaism. And it is unsurprising that these rabbis were keen to describe their accession to authorized status as being much smoother than it may in fact have been.

Another problem is the very persistence of this Jewish Christian voice long after it was supposed to have disappeared. In the 1960s, the great Jewish scholar Shlomo Pines came across an Islamic text of the late tenth century attributed to a Muslim theologian, Abd al-Jabbar. This text describes the resentments of a Jewish Christian community who argued that the mainstream Christian community, under the malign influence of St Paul, had abandoned the religion of Jesus, abandoned the Mosaic law, and adopted the alien customs of the Romans in order to gain power and influence. In essence, they argued, the mainstream Gentile Christians, the Bnei Noah, had sold out to the Romans, the very people who had crucified Christ in the first place. The text is thick with scurrilous accounts of monks and priests who had committed apostasy and defected to the enemy, the evil Romans. And, they argued, the Emperor Constantine was a leper. This tenth-century document seems to provide evidence of the existence of Jewish Christian communities long after they were supposed to have been declared impossible. In Shlomo Pines's view, these communities appear to have sheltered under the protection of early Islam.

Whatever one makes of this example, it is pretty clear that there were Jewish Christian communities long after they were supposed to have been declared invalid, by both the Gentile Christian Church and by rabbinic Jews. Indeed, the fact that both Jews and early Christian writers of the second and third centuries return again and again to the theme of attacking Jewish Christians is itself evidence that they persisted long past Yavneh.

The problem with the whole Yavneh 'parting of the ways' model is that it assumes that there was an accepted authority that was able to adjudicate and make such a separation official. But, of course, that is precisely what is at stake in these centuries. The language of heresy and orthodoxy, the demarcation of what counts as official religion, is a highly contested business. Moreover, if there is no such thing as an agreed version of Judaism, indeed if the very idea of Judaism as being a 'religion' is a much later construct (as I am about to argue), then what can we mean by people leaving, or being expelled from, Judaism during the first century?

No, it was the Romans who imposed official boundaries on Christianity. In the fourth century, Roman Christianity drew on Roman imperial authority to settle the question of who was and who was not a member of the Church. But despite this, there have always been those who have rejected the way the Romans – whether based in Rome or Constantinople – brokered the official version of Christianity, the terms of which would have been invidious to the early Jesus movement. There have long been unofficial versions of Christianity and Judaism – and Jewish Christianity, Christianity's original form, ended up becoming one such minority report.

9

Being Jewish is linked to geography and to genealogical origin in a way that being Christian is not. Modern ideas of race are not helpful here – not least, of course, because 'scientific' racism was itself constructed as a form of antisemitism. In the first century, Jewish group identity was an unspecified combination of who your parents and grandparents were, where you came from geographically, and which customs you followed. Being Jewish was, and remains, more about ethnicity, place, custom and belonging; being Christian more about belief. In other words, the innate grammar of the words 'Christian' and 'Jewish' are of a completely different shape and behave in completely different ways.

Another way of putting this would be as follows. Until Christianity, there was no such thing as religion – that is, no such thing as a separate body of instruction about God(s), no such thing as a set of practices distinct from who your grandparents are or where you were brought up. Before Christianity, the gods that people believed in were traditionally the gods of their people. Yahweh was the God of the Jews. Dagon was the god of the Philistines. Baal was the god of the Canaanites.

The worship of Yahweh was thus not detachable from being a Jew. That is why, for instance, the Bible contains no specific word for Judaism. And this is important. In Judaism, beliefs, doctrines, etc. are not the organizing principles. Indeed, according to the Jewish Talmudic scholar Daniel Boyarin, Jews began to use the word 'Judaism' in the way we use it today only well into the eighteenth century. Before then, the idea of there being a separate name for some sort of religion or set of beliefs that could be described independently of genealogical identity didn't make much sense. There was no such thing as Judaism as a doctrine that Jews believed in.

Rather it was Pauline Christianity, precisely because it abandoned the idea of faith as an expression of ethnicity and culture, that invented the idea of there being such a thing as religion or faith made up of a set of distinct beliefs and practices. For some, therefore, the word 'religion' – even the word 'Judaism' itself – is worryingly Christian in the way it functions. We continue to use such words as a convenience because sentences become incredibly clunky otherwise – for example my use of the term 'Jesus-following Jews' instead of Christians – but words like 'Christianity' and 'Judaism' come with the warning that they are not native terms and that inscribed within their etymology are traces of a way of understanding the world that are distinctly Christian. As a consequence, the assumptions of this world view can be very distorting.

Boyarin offers the following highly illuminating example. Before the British invaded India there was no such religion as Hinduism. The British felt that they needed a name for the whole array of practices, cults, beliefs, gods, etc. that they came across in India, so they gave it one. 'Hinduism' was not a term native to India before the British Empire demanded that there be one. The British expected that a 'religion' must have a collection of sacred scriptures, like the Bible, and this expectation became an organizing principle. But only a tiny minority of middle-class 'Hindus' had ever heard of the Bhagavad-Gita or the Vedas until well into the eighteenth century – until, that is, the British translated them and basically informed the Hindus that this was to be their equivalent of the Bible.

We saw in the previous chapter how the British expected a religion to be organized with some sort of titular head, like a pope or an archbishop. Hence the encouragement the British Jews received to establish something equivalent to meet this expectation – and the very British invention of the Chief Rabbinate. Everywhere the British wanted to find a reliable interlocutor, a head man and a set of rules. The assumptions made about what a religion ought to look like by the Christian-minded British Empire shaped the ways in which they treated the 'religions' of India and the ways in which these 'religions' then developed under British rule.

All of this is important because, when it comes to considering the 'religious' practices and beliefs of Jews and Christians in the first century of the Christian era, we must be conscious that the sort of taxonomy that the modern consciousness has come to expect may not be found there at all. We must beware of imposing modern distinctions on a period that would have had no use for them.

Why all these warnings? Because I have been trying to tell a story about the early centuries of what came to be called Christianity that cuts against many deeply ingrained expectations. It is a counter-narrative to the one that has long been promoted by the dominant imperial power of the first centuries of the so-called Christian era. Like the British in India, the Romans played with the boundaries of what counted as Christianity in such a way as to obscure the fact that the Jesus-followers began as a movement of, by and for Jews. To put it bluntly: just as the British Empire invented Hinduism, so the Roman Empire invented Christianity.

10.

Finally, let me return to the Rebbe and to David Berger's reaction to the Meshichistim. For it was Berger's book that inspired the comparison I have made between the Rebbe and Jesus. Why was David Berger so exercised by what he calls the 'scandal of orthodox indifference' to the messianic claims being made about the Rebbe? The answer he gives is clear: 'I lay awake for many hours asking myself how this was possible, whether the stand of generations of Jewish polemicists against Christianity was being summarily discarded.' And again, 'our children will no longer be able to tell Christian missionaries that the Jewish faith does not countenance belief in a Messiah whose mission is interrupted by death, and one of the defining characteristics of Judaism in a Christian world will have been erased'.

Berger invokes Jewish 'orthodoxy' so as to protect the boundaries between Christianity and Judaism, specifically to protect Judaism from the incursion of Christian missionaries. He takes the famous disputation of Nachmanides – the so-called Barcelona Disputation of 1263 – as representative of Jewish polemics as a whole. The essence of Nachmanides' argument is that Jesus cannot have been the Messiah because he did not achieve what the Bible said he ought to have achieved: the earth was not filled with the glory of God following his mission. Swords were not beaten into ploughshares. War and death did not end. Jesus failed. Most important of all, he died. In other words, 'Jesus cannot be the Messiah because the prophecies of the messianic age have not been fulfilled.' He relates the story of Rabbi Chaim Soloveitchik of Brisk outsmarting a Christian missionary by getting him to admit that Simon bar Kokhba could not have been the Messiah because he was killed by the Romans before he fulfilled his mission to redeem the people of Israel. In other words, neither Jesus nor Simon (nor the Rebbe) could have been the Messiah because they all failed to achieve the messianic mission.

It is highly significant that the historical examples he draws on as evidence for the hostility of traditional Judaism to the messianism of the Meshichistim are taken from the Middle Ages, when the very existence of Judaism was under threat from Christian aggression and enforced conversion. For Berger, orthodoxy exists to protect Judaism from attack. And that too was the reason the early rabbis drew a fence around the Torah. Fences protect. Given the bloody history of the twentieth century, it is hard not to sympathize with Berger's desire to defend the ramparts of Jewish identity.

It is out of respect for this position that I remain suspicious of messianic Judaism. Jews for Jesus is a proselytizing organization that seeks the conversion of Jews to Christianity. The embrace that Jews for Jesus have for fellow Jews, dressed up as concern for their immortal souls, is in effect one that would lead to the destruction of a specifically Jewish culture that has been under threat for centuries. And I will not align myself with that. Furthermore, if what I have argued is correct, then Jews for Jesus shouldn't really be proselytizing at all – at least, if they are seeking to remain true to the religion of the first Jewish Christians. The Jewish Christians of the Jerusalem Church didn't especially prioritize conversion. That was St Paul's priority. He turned Jesus into a global franchise.

I know I risk being misunderstood. I do not mean to disparage St Paul or the enormous contribution he made to the development of the Christian story. Rather, I have attempted to try to imagine Christianity from the lost perspective of Jewish Christianity – and that has required me to muscle in some intellectual space. Those who think I have been unfair on Paul are probably right. Christianity ended up as a globalized phenomenon and Judaism retained its rootedness in the specifics of place and ethnicity. They stand in relationship to each other as 'Somewheres' do to 'Anywheres', to borrow the journalist David Goodhart's telling distinction. My own ghosts make me more predisposed to the Somewheres than a Christian priest probably ought to be. It's not Jews but Christians who are the real 'rootless cosmopolitans', to use a phrase often levelled against Jews. And this is a tension that I will just have to live with. But not all tensions need resolving: some just need to be borne – perhaps even celebrated.

In his ground-breaking *A Radical Jew: Paul and the Politics of Identity* (1994), Daniel Boyarin makes a fascinating point about the respective and contrasting merits of Christianity and Judaism: 'The genius of Christianity is its concern for all of the peoples of the world; the genius of rabbinic Judaism is its ability to leave other people alone.' But precisely because of its concern for all people, the genius of Christianity has a shadow side: 'The very emphasis on a universalism expressed as concern for all of the families of the world turns very rapidly (if not necessarily) into a doctrine that they must all become part of our family of the spirit, with all the horrifying practices against Jews and other Others which Christian Europe produced.' In other words, whereas Judaism maintains the importance of difference, Christianity insists on a 'coercive sameness'. The shadow side of Judaism is an indifference to non-Jews, 'as the Palestinians know only too well,' Boyarin asserts, 'but Christian universalism has been historically even more dangerous'.

II.

For the first few months after I arrived in my new job as the parish priest of St Mary, Newington, at the Elephant and Castle in south London, I assumed that half of the congregation must have come from one extended family. Why else would so many be calling each other 'auntie' or 'uncle'? It took me ages to twig that this was a way in which many people with West African origins often express a kind of spiritual unity with each other. To be 'auntie' or 'uncle' was to be a part of the extended family – which is also why so many in my congregation insist on calling me 'Father Giles'. In this Christian family, all can belong. Water is thicker than blood – that is, the water of baptism is thicker than the blood of biological inheritance. Jesus was often pretty mean about his own biological family: 'Who are my brother and sister?' he questioned. 'Whoever does the will of my father in heaven is my brother and sister.' It was in the name of this universal family that missionaries set out to convert the world, to make all into one.

That, of course, is Boyarin's point. The genius of Christianity is its capacity for multiculturalism. The great danger is Christianity's desire for it.

5. Temple

I.

> When the day of Pentecost had come, they were all together in one place. And suddenly from heaven there came a sound like the rush of a violent wind, and it filled the entire house where they were sitting. Divided tongues, as of fire, appeared among them, and a tongue rested on each of them. All of them were filled with the Holy Spirit . . . (Acts 2: 1–3)

The second chapter of the Book of Acts describes an extraordinary event that was said to have taken place during the festival of Pentecost. Jews from all over the diaspora had journeyed up to Jerusalem to celebrate their harvest festival. 'God fearing Jews from every nation under heaven' is how Acts describes them. NB: it says Jews.

'Pentecost' sounds like a Christian word, being derived from the Greek word for 'fifty', but this obscures the Jewish nature of what is going on here. 'Pentecost' is a Greek word because many Jews of the diaspora spoke Greek, often as their first language. A good many didn't understand much Hebrew at all. Following the conquests of Alexander the Great during the late fourth century BC, Greek became the lingua franca of many international Jews – the first books of the Hebrew Bible having already been translated into Greek sometime around the third century BCE.

The number fifty is particularly significant in this story because it represents the day after seven weeks (7 x 7) after

Passover. In Hebrew, the festival is known as Shavuot, after the Hebrew word for seven, *sheva*. And like all biblical references to seven, it is code for the seven days of creation when the breath (*ruach*) of God (variously translated, also as 'wind' or 'spirit'), the life-giving force, is imparted to all that God has made. It is as if God breathes creation into being. The term *ruach* or spirit, is there at the very opening of the Bible: 'The Spirit [*ruach*] of God was hovering over the surface of the waters' (Genesis 1:2). The Jewish harvest festival of Pentecost was thus a kind of festival of creation. As the wheat and barley were gathered in from the fields, so the best of this life-giving harvest, the fruits of creation, were taken to the Temple and offered back to God as thanksgiving. 'For all things come from you, and of your own have we given you,' as the Book of Chronicles puts it.

The date is important to this story, but so is the place. Jerusalem is where the gap between heaven and earth is said to be at its thinnest, the place where God's life force – His *ruach* – might most easily make the leap from heaven to earth. Imagine it as a bit like an electrostatic charge that jumps between the globes of a Van de Graaff generator. In the excitable atmosphere of a packed Jerusalem, tongues of flame were said to have descended on the followers of Jesus, enabling them miraculously to talk in a language that was understandable to everyone, no matter where they came from.

For later Christians, Pentecost came to be imagined as the beginnings of religious multiculturalism. The sermon goes like this: whatever our original culture, whatever our linguistic differences, the spirit of God can transcend them, speaking directly to all. In the Christian imagination, Pentecost morphed from a Jewish harvest festival into a celebration of Christian universalism. The specific culture in which one was raised no longer mattered, the sermon continues. Jews or Greeks, Libyans, Parthians or Medes, God could bypass all of that. Pentecost is often described as the birthday of the Church. In Christian culture, this has become a way of telling the story of how the Christian 'Anywheres' established their theological dominance over the Jewish 'Somewheres'. Or, to put it rather simplistically: how Judaism went global and became Christianity. But that is not really the story here at all. For what is going on at Pentecost is not so much the birth of something new, as the continuation of something very old, a very Jewish answer to a very Jewish problem. Pentecost is the story of God jumping the distance between Himself and humanity.

2.

Strict monotheism, often understood as the defining feature of ancient Judaism, presents what one might call a plumbing problem – or, to put it less colloquially, a problem of mediation: how are human beings connected with God? We could pose the question in a more philosophical way: how is a transcendent God that is separate from His creation also a God that is involved with it? This problem reflects two powerful yet strongly divergent instincts about the divine. First, that God is wholly other, transcendent, above and beyond. Indeed, God is so different that He exists in a completely different kind of way from all that He has made. It's not just physical difference that separates heaven and earth but, as it were, ontological difference. God and humanity have different kinds of being. Sitting alongside this, however, is the equally powerful idea that God comes close to humanity and is intimately involved with all that He has made. God is present, and in some sense knowable and experienceable.

Different religious traditions balance these instincts in their own individual ways – some emphasize the transcendent, some the immanent. But none of them can entirely do away with the other. And as such, all religious traditions are built on what seems like a philosophical contradiction. How is it possible for God to be both wholly other yet intimately present?

I suggest that this is a central preoccupation of the Bible. And when seen from this perspective it becomes considerably easier to appreciate both the continuity and discontinuity between the Old Testament and the New. This perspective also helps us appreciate why the various ways of addressing this same problem are unstable, constantly threatened by the inherent contradiction of holding together two things that cannot be held together, and therefore constantly on the point of collapsing into new ways of solving the unsolvable.

The Temple, for instance, was one way of addressing the plumbing problem, which is why it is sometimes known as 'the navel of the earth' – an umbilical cord linking God and humanity. The incarnation was another version of the same thing. To put it in Christian terms, the Temple is seen as a kind of incarnation – God's presence on earth, and so the Christian idea of the incarnation can be seen, amongst other things, as an extension of the theology of the Temple as first expressed in the Hebrew Scriptures. As a result, after the destruction of the Temple in CE 70, the transference of Temple theology to the person of Jesus was an obvious move for early Christians to make. Jesus was the new Temple, they argued. Temple theology provided a ready-made answer to the plumbing problem, and this was appropriated by early Christians and reused to understand the role of Jesus himself, the new high priest. This is how Christian reflection on the person of Jesus 'emerged so rapidly and with such a high degree of definition', as the theologian Margaret Barker puts it. In other words, the theology was already there, just waiting to be lifted and reapplied.

3.

There are various ways in which the plumbing problem is tackled in the Hebrew Scriptures. One of the most obvious is by postulating intermediaries like angels, shuttling back and forth between heaven and earth. These liminal, semi-divine figures communicate God to humanity, and intercede with God on humanity's behalf. Angels are classic intermediaries, 'messengers' literally translated, with one foot in heaven, one on earth – avatars of God, as it were. And yet, despite the fact that angels are constantly referenced throughout the Old Testament, the very existence of these liminal messenger-type figures presents a particular challenge to the basic assumptions of strict monotheism within the Hebrew Scriptures.

Daniel, chapter 7, for instance, is especially challenging for strict monotheism. In this justifiably famous passage, an older God, the so-called 'Ancient of Days', is imagined sitting on a throne, with thousands and thousands of worshippers before him. Also present appears to be a younger divinity known as the 'son of man':

> To him was given dominion and glory and kingship, that all peoples, nations and languages should serve him. His dominion is an everlasting dominion that shall not pass away, and his kingdom is one that shall never be destroyed. (Daniel 7:14)

This 'son of man' tradition is developed in a number of passages elsewhere in Jewish and early Christian literature.

The book of Enoch, for example, though not included in most of the canons of the Jewish or Christian Bible, was written sometime in the later part of the first century and indicates the persistence of this 'son of man' idea. 'And there I saw One who had a head of days, and His head was white like wool, and with Him was another being, whose countenance had the appearance of a man, and his face was full of graciousness.' This is a riff on Daniel 7, and suggests the endurance of the idea of a second redeemer-type figure, clearly quasi-divine, that sits alongside God the Father, the Ancient of Days. All of this poses an enormous challenge to traditional Jewish self-understanding, coming as it does perilously close to denying the founding proposition of Jewish theology: that divinity is irreducibly singular. Margaret Barker makes the point provocatively in the subtitle of her book *The Great Angel: A Study of Israel's Second God*.

Another, not dissimilar strategy for addressing the plumbing problem is more abstract and philosophical. Instead of postulating the existence of mythological and personified intermediaries, those writers who were more influenced by Greek thought – and particularly by that of Plato, Pythagoras and the Stoics – developed the idea that reason provided the connection, the plumbing. For the Stoics, reason – or the Logos – was the animating and fundamentally generative principle of the entire universe. Human beings were linked with this animating principle because it permeated all things. For the Stoics, the Logos was the thing that connected up the one and the many, the unifying basis of all life in which humanity participated.

The Jewish Greek-speaking philosopher and theologian Philo of Alexandria argues the case for this unifying connection. Born some twenty or so years before the birth of Christ, and a resident of Egypt, Philo is just the sort of Jew of the diaspora that the story of Pentecost had in mind. Philo's God is also thoroughly transcendent, and Philo, like Plato, refuses any of the traditional anthropomorphisms that made God more human and thus more approachable. His version of the plumbing problem is thus particularly acute, and he attempts to solve it through the Logos, as Maren Niehoff demonstrates in his book of 2018, *Philo of Alexandria: An Intellectual Biography*:

> Philo's Logos theology thus emerges in a thoroughly Alexandrian context with its characteristic orientation toward Platonic and Pythagorean ideas. It provides an answer to the question of how the utterly transcendent God can have been involved in the creation. Sensitive to the diverse meanings of the word 'Logos', which range from concrete items such as a book to abstract rationality, Philo attributes central importance to this concept and constructs it as an ideal mediator between the material and the ethereal realms.

Interestingly, Philo first introduces his idea of Logos in the context of a discussion of the significance of the number seven – which, as mentioned previously, is Jewish code for the work of creation. Combining Genesis with the Pythagorean idea that a mathematical structure permeates the universe, Philo posits an affinity that the number seven has with the Logos – thus connecting mind via abstract reason to the material creation it pervades. The Logos becomes an epistemological link between an absent God and human reality.

In the hands of the author of John's Gospel – who was writing perhaps a century later – this Logos/spirit/mind/life-force combination also held a remarkable affinity with the breath of God described in the opening verses of Genesis. Thus the famous opening of John's Gospel, beloved of Christmas carol services: 'In the beginning was the Word

[Logos] and the Word was with God, and the Word was God.' With its deliberate reference to the opening passage in Genesis, this is also the language of the creation. John goes on to describe this Logos being made flesh in the person of Jesus. Cleverly merging the Jewish tradition of the spirit of God with the Greek-inspired idea of Logos, John presents the appearance of the Messiah Jesus as the ultimate answer to the plumbing problem. By doing this, he explicitly pushes Christian theology in the direction of the Trinity – that God is both one and more than one at the same time. In other words, though Jews would later come to disparage the doctrine of the Trinity as something deeply antithetical to Judaism, the roots of trinitarian thinking can be traced back to a problem that the Hebrew Scriptures had been struggling with from the very beginning.

Drawing together threads from deep within the Jewish tradition, the idea of Trinity is a combination of God the Father, the white-bearded Ancient of Days God; the younger God the Son, the 'one like a Son of Man' that gets mapped on to the person of Jesus, the Messiah; and the Holy Spirit God, the mediator, the connector, the Logos, infusing all creation. In very basic terms, the Trinity is the Jewish God who is wholly Other, plus Jewish messianic expectation believed to be realized in the person of Jesus, plus the Holy Spirit (*ruach*). The Trinity is the Christian solution to the plumbing problem.

4.

One important element is still missing here, though we have touched on it. For of all the various ancient answers to this problem, the most important was probably the institution of the Temple itself. Built by King Solomon at the high point of Jewish pride and power, roughly a thousand years before the birth of Christ, the First Temple was an extraordinary building project, with tens of thousands of labourers conscripted to bring cedar and cypress wood from Lebanon and cut stone from quarries. Roughly the size of an Olympic swimming pool, this was the place where the Ark of the Covenant would be housed. The Ark contained the tablets of stone originally handed down to Moses by God on Mount Sinai, and was initially carried around in a tent, reflecting the peripatetic existence of a people yet to find their home. The establishment of the First Temple was significant in representing a settled existence in the Promised Land.

The Ark was placed in the centre of the Temple, in the holiest of holies, surrounded by two large statues of cherubim with outstretched arms, made of wood and covered in gold. Two huge pillars of bronze – named Boaz and Jachin – stood either side of the heavy olive-wood carved door to the holiest of holies. This was the hub of the universe. In a courtyard around the Temple, washstands were set up for ritual washing and altars were established for the people to make and bring sacrifices to their God. The divine had finally found His proper dwelling place on earth. Solomon built his personal palace next to the Temple, reflecting the important connection between divinity and kingship, the latter claiming its authority from the former. When adherents to the Messiahking tradition seek to 'make Israel great again', this is the period they hark back to.

This golden period was to prove short-lived, however. Soon after Solomon, political intrigue and international intervention divided up the united kingdoms of Judah and Israel, and with this division the question was raised whether the declining fortunes of the Jewish people was somehow linked to a failure of plumbing – whether the intimate connection between God and His people, made through the Temple, had somehow come to be blocked. This troubling idea became an obsession that dominates much of the Hebrew Scriptures – in the book of Ezekiel, God's glory is described as having departed the Temple. It was a national disaster. This is what the book of Lamentations was lamenting about. This is what made Jeremiah so miserable. And all agreed that the flourishing of God's chosen people could only be re-established once God had returned and the plumbing problem had been sorted out.

It is not too much of an overstatement to say that the question of what made God leave the Temple, and how to bring Him back, became the driving force of the theology of the Hebrew Scriptures. Did God leave because the Temple was desecrated? Had the people become faithless? Was the sacrificial practice not being done right? Did the Temple need reform? Had sin infected the Temple? Impurity? Corruption? Were too many foreign practices being introduced into Temple worship? One line of thought, expressed by later rabbis, marks the beginning of the end as the very day when the Temple was consecrated, for this was also the day that Solomon married the daughter of the Egyptian Pharaoh. In this line of thought, the marrying of foreign wives, and thus the proximity of an alien religion to God's dwelling place, was the reason God fled the Temple. I will return to this question in the next chapter.

Roughly speaking, there are two broad categories of solutions offered as to how our relationship to God gets blocked. The first answer is that the plumbing gets blocked for cultic reasons – that is, by the introduction of alien elements into the system. These alien elements include the presence of some sort of impurity, be that the proximity of foreign gods or their acolytes, including foreign wives, or the violation of the various distinctions – food laws, purity regulations concerning the proximity to death and various bodily processes – that were intended to maintain the distinctiveness of the Jewish cult and thus exclude outside interventions.

Explaining the significance of purity regulations concerning dead bodies, semen and menstrual blood remains a controversial topic, though many find the explanation of American scholar Rabbi Jacob Milgrom convincing: that the most basic of theological associations is of God with life itself. From this perspective, purity regulations are intended to keep God as far apart as possible from the contaminating presence of death in all its various forms. Corpses and diseased bodies suggest some challenge to the super-abundance of life that is God. Likewise, semen is regarded as contaminating because, unless employed directly in the reproductive process, it symbolizes a lost opportunity for life, thus an indication of death. But the tricky thing about Milgrom's 'impurity-as-death' idea is that the Temple is actually the place where animal sacrifice is made, and so absolutely a place of death. If Milgrom was right, wouldn't animal sacrifice itself be defiling the Temple?

Perhaps the answer to this puzzle may be something like this: that animal sacrifice is not so much about death and decay itself, but rather it is a representation of a full and perfect life returned to God as an honour to its creator; that sacrifice is some sort of ritualized acknowledgement that the power and oversight concerning life and death is, properly speaking God's business. 'The Lord kills and brings to life' (1 Samuel 2:6). In other words, it is God that has the power over life and death, and His authority in these matters must not be taken into human hands.

The second category of answer is more straightforward:

that the plumbing gets blocked for broadly moral reasons; in particular, that the priests of the Temple have been corrupted by money and/or power and/or sex. Thus, for instance, Amos (2:8) attacks the Temple cult for its general debauchery and economic exploitation: 'They lay themselves down beside every altar on garments taken in pledge; and in the house of their God they drink wine bought with fines they imposed.' This is in the tradition of Temple critique from which Jesus speaks when he throws the money-changers out of the Temple precincts. It is not, as it is sometimes erroneously understood, a specifically 'Christian' attack on the very idea of the Temple. Jesus' critique exists in a long tradition of Jewish polemic against Temple corruption.

So, again broadly speaking, the first answer as to how things get blocked comes from the priests and those who write in the priestly tradition. Their answer sees the problem as a failure to properly implement the cultic regulations. The second answer is the answer of the prophets – the problem here being a moral one. Both categories reference a form of self-forgetfulness; that the Temple and its functionaries have turned away from God and become more interested in something else.

5.

Now let me come clean about one of the things that this chapter is all about. For although I have strayed a long way from my discussion of Occupy and its impact on St Paul's Cathedral, that has remained very much at the back of my mind as I have ventured into the complex theology of the early formation of Christianity.

In December 2011, the Corporation of London proceeded

to the High Court to secure the eviction of the Occupy protesters still camped on the forecourt of St Paul's Cathedral. The legal ownership of the land on which the protesters had pitched their tents was uncertain – it was owned either by St Paul's or by the Corporation of London – and resolving such ancient issues of title was expected to take a considerable amount of time. To expedite matters swiftly, both groups had to act together, which was why the eviction proceedings, although driven by the Corporation, needed the express support of the cathedral authorities. And this support came in the form of a submission to the Court, outlining the reasons that the cathedral felt it must forcibly clear the protesters from its steps. Among the various reasons for eviction, Major General Nicholas Cottam, the Registrar of the Cathedral, wrote this: 'Human defecation has occurred in the west portico entrance and inside the cathedral on several occasions.'

It seems that, on one occasion, a homeless woman, confused and embarrassed, had an accident and evacuated her bowels within the cathedral. The protesters later explained to me that this poor woman had mental-health issues, and she was looking for help. But to many of the cathedral staff, defecation on the well-polished marble floor was interpreted as an attack, a deliberate insult. More than any other incident throughout the months of the Occupy protest, it was probably this pile of poo that polarized opinion the most. It was unpleasant to clear up, of course. But this wasn't really the issue. At stake here was something surprisingly theological – in Christian terms, what is the proper relationship between a church and the messiness of the world? Does the church seek to maintain and protect a cordoned-off sanctuary of purity, a pollution-free space for a pollution-free God? Or is the whole point of the incarnation that God becomes human, thus collapsing the barriers between the sacred and the profane, between God and shit? This cut to the core of what a church should be all about. And, as a theological question, it is a variant of the plumbing problem.

Now you may think me totally mad, but it was this single act of defecation that has driven the puzzle and anguish behind a great deal of the theology of this book. It is not too much to say that it has obsessed me. In my head, it came to stand for all the differences that were there between the clergy with respect to Occupy. For some of us, the question of Occupy was a moral one – about banks and economics and social justice. It was these things that, as it were, interfered with the connection between God and humanity. It was here that St Paul's had failed – and the protesters were like prophets, calling us out for our complicity with a system that had placed Mammon before God. From this perspective, the presence of shit within the cathedral ought to be cleaned up quickly, without fuss, and understood ideologically in terms of the unfortunate circumstances of the woman herself. Cleaning up after her should be recognized as a part of Christian servant leadership and a preferential option for the poor and the marginalized.

But there were also those, I believe, who understood Occupy very differently. Their presence – symbolized by this act of defecation – became a sort of ritual pollution; at the very least a disruption to the connection the cathedral was there to make between God and humanity. Both sides understood Occupy as pointing to, or itself representing, a blockage of the divine plumbing. Was the problem ritual or moral?

To those who may think that this is simply a very niche, obscure and obsolete dispute among the clergy, I want to suggest that it has a surprising contemporary relevance. A few weeks after Major Cottam made his case for the eviction of Occupy at the High Court, the social psychologist

Jonathan Haidt published the hugely influential *The Righteous Mind*, a book that sought to explain the appeal of political conservatism to liberals who found it incomprehensible. At the heart of Haidt's explanation is that conservatives employ a more extensive palate of political values, including and in particular a cluster of values like purity and disgust. This, Haidt contends, is one of those divisive set of values that the right employs – to powerful electoral effect – but liberals denigrate and misunderstand.

Yuck reflexes are powerful without being obviously rational. For example, we all have saliva in our mouths. But most of us would recoil if asked to spit in a glass and then drink it. There seems no apparent reason for us to react with such disgust at being asked to drink our own spit and yet also be so completely relaxed about the same material circulating in our mouths. When this type of powerful visceral reaction is seen in the context of ethics, the liberal compass wavers. On the one hand, liberals rightly fear the application of this sort of gut reaction to issues such as sexuality and race – to the idea that gay sex is disgusting or that there is 'something wrong' about the idea of mixed-race couples. The absence of rationality in these reactions is rightly understood to be indicative of prejudice.

But consider this. Is there anything morally wrong with (to take a grotesque example) having sex with a dead chicken in the privacy of one's own kitchen (or bedroom?) – not one specifically killed for the purpose, but one purchased at the supermarket? Strictly from the perspective of the liberal world view, where harm is typically understood as the deciding moral factor, there doesn't seem to be anything obviously wrong with this. After all, what or who is harmed in the act? Yet the sense that there is indeed something wrong here would be a common reaction. Is this, too, simply prejudice?

The anthropologist Mary Douglas has written powerfully and persuasively about disgust and purity as a moral reaction. For her, the nature of impurity only makes sense in terms of a world view in which things are assigned a certain place, and an impure substance is not, in and of itself, impure – it is simply in the wrong place. Saliva is not disgusting in the mouth, but is disgusting in a glass. Dirt is a good thing in the garden, but a bad thing when trampled through the house. In other words, impurity and disgust are context-dependent – even faeces. Its presence in one's intestine is not generally something one reacts to with disgust, nor – for the most part – in the toilet bowl. But on the floor of a cathedral, that is a different matter. And here is the big point: disgust and purity only make sense with reference to a sort of map of the world in which things have their proper place.

The phrase 'a place for everything and everything in its place' – often associated with Benjamin Franklin – has its origin in a religious world view. 'The Lord hath set everything in its place and order,' preached Bishop John Hacket in 1675. The phrase as we know it is probably a popular Victorian rendition of this religious idea. God sets things in a certain order during the seven days of creation. Disgust is a gut reaction to things not being as God has set them up to be, or – in a secular rendition of the same basic idea – as nature intended.

There can, for instance, be similar secular and religious reactions to some experiments in genetics. It may well be that there is no obviously discernible harm in splicing together the genes of different species in order to produce, say, more biologically resilient forms of life. Nonetheless, there is often a gut feeling that such experiments are 'wrong' in so far as they do not respect the proper order of things. I would suggest that the big difference between liberal and conservative instincts is to be found here: liberals generally do not have a sense of there being a 'proper order of things' that should be respected. Conservatives do.

What liberals often don't understand is that the desire for a world in which everything has a proper place is a reaction to a radically uncertain world, a world in which boundaries have been effaced, and thus a world in which nothing is protected, no one is safe – especially the most vulnerable. To those, for instance, who have been on the rough end of global capitalism – the greatest change agent the world has ever known and a battering ram of liberal freedom – this desire for protection, a need for the world to contain deep-rooted barriers, can run extremely deep.

This returns us to the Temple. For many writers of the first century, the Temple was to be understood as a kind of map of the universe, an expression of how God had ordered things at the time of the creation. In other words, the Temple functioned as a representation of the place where things were supposed to exist in God's created order – an order that was, as much as anything, about the maintenance of justice and peace. According to Jewish historian Josephus, the purpose of the Temple was 'to recall and represent the universe'. For him, the division of the Temple into three distinct areas – the outer courtyard, the holy space and the holiest of holies – was a symbolic representation of the division of the world into earth and sea and heaven, the first two being generally acceptable to human beings, the third space being the preserve of God. Others have indicated the significance of the fact that the veil of the Temple, the heavy woven fabric through which the holy of holies was accessed, was woven with images of birds and trees – again, a portrayal of the created order.

Likewise, Philo, who we have already seen was particularly

concerned to establish connection between God and humanity, argues that 'The highest, and in the truest sense the holy, temple of God is, as we must believe, the whole universe.' Indeed, Philo goes on to describe in great detail the cosmic symbolism of the ritual clothes worn by Temple priests. For Philo, these Temple priests were, one might say, wearing the world on their shoulders. They were doing on earth an equivalent job to that performed by angels in heaven. All of which is a symbolic representation of Philo's answer to the plumbing problem. The high priest, for example, is 'endowed with a nature higher than the merely human and to approximate the Divine, on the borderline, we may truly say, between the two, that people may have a mediator through whom they may propitiate God and God a subordinate to employ in extending the abundance of his boons to men'.

The Temple, then, is the place where God and humanity reach out to each other, and this reaching out is established through some sense of correspondence between the Temple and the cosmos. The Temple models creation and thus brings heaven and earth into alignment. Once this alignment is established, a portal is opened up between God and humanity. That is why the foundation stone of the world was said to have been located within the sanctuary of the Temple, as explained in this well-known rabbinic midrash:

Just as the navel is the centre of a person, so the Land of Israel is the navel of the earth (Ezekiel 38:12). The land of Israel sits at the centre of the world, Jerusalem at the centre of the land of Israel, the Temple in the centre of Jerusalem, the sanctuary at the centre of the Temple, the ark in the centre of sanctuary, and the foundation stone – from which the world was formed – sits in front of the sanctuary. (Midrash Tanchuma, Kedoshim 10:2)

It is now easier to recognize how this theology is very directly lifted from Jewish theology and applied to the person of Christ. Consider, for instance, this passage where Paul (or one of his close disciples) is writing to the Ephesians, expressing the typically Pauline view that, in Christ, the division between Jew and Gentile has been torn down.

> So then you are no longer strangers and aliens, but you are citizens with the saints and also members of the household of God, built upon the foundation of the apostles and prophets, with Christ Jesus as the cornerstone. In him the whole structure is joined together and grows into a holy temple in the Lord. (Ephesians 2:19)

In his brilliant little book, *The Temple of Jerusalem*, Simon Goldhill has argued that after the destruction of the Temple, it was the Christians who continued to maintain much of its distinctive theology, albeit in a mutated form. Jesus may have railed against the Temple, predicting its downfall, condemning its abuses in the manner of the Hebrew prophets before him, but he also supplied a central metaphor that guaranteed its ongoing significance in the life of Christianity. Jews may lament the destruction of the Temple and look for the day that it will be rebuilt with the coming of the Messiah. But Jesus – the person Christians recognize as the Messiah – supplies a much more immediate answer. The Temple will be destroyed, Jesus predicts, but it will be raised up again. 'Destroy this temple and in three days I will raise it up' (John 2:19). This is a reference to the resurrection, of course. With Jesus' resurrection a new Temple will be born: the resurrected Jesus is himself the new Temple. The Temple thus transmutes from architecture to flesh and blood. The person of Jesus is a continuation of the theological role of the Temple, the new answer to the plumbing problem.

St Paul goes further: 'your body is a temple', he famously claimed. This phrase, the meaning of which is often over-shadowed by health-nuts who want to claim it as advice for healthy living, should be understood much more specifically. The Church is the 'body of Christ', and this body is an exten-sion of the Temple. Palestinian Christians living in Bethlehem can be scathing about the busloads of tourists who nervously enter the West Bank to make their way to see Constantine the Great's Church of the Nativity in Manger Square, often ignoring the existence of the actual Christians who live there. That these tourists are more concerned with the dead stones of architecture than with the 'living stones' of the church is a familiar critique. The church isn't the building – it's the people. These Palestinian Christians have a point: Christians shouldn't fetishize their buildings.

Of course buildings are, for some, a crucial part of their connection with God. When the Archbishop of Canterbury, Justin Welby, asked Church of England clergy not to pray, even on their own, in their churches during the Covid-19 pandemic, he triggered a row in the Church between those for whom the church building is an important part of how God is made present to them, and those for whom it is a burdensome pile of bricks, no more than a glorified rain shelter. Like many theological rows, the reason people get exercised is that what is at stake here is the way people make contact with God. The conduits may change, but their func-tion remains remarkably similar. Thus the reference to 'living stones' is a shift of Temple theology over to the people of God, the Church. Christianity did not suddenly invent a whole new theology in the first century: it borrowed and reapplied it. There is little that is new in the New Testament.

6

Nonetheless, despite St Paul's transference of Temple theology from stones to people, there is a long tradition of Christian churches borrowing from the architectural grammar of the Jerusalem Temple. The sanctuary of many Christian churches, for instance – the holy bit protected by an altar rail – is a direct descendant of the walled divisions of the Temple that separated off the holy and the profane. Medieval churches often constructed altar screens, visually blocking the holy activity of the Eucharist from the gaze of hoi polloi. This division runs surprisingly deep and remains central to Orthodox churches, of course. It explains that frisson of unease that is commonly experienced when, for instance, a small child with sticky paws breaks free from his mother and runs up into the sanctuary. It is as if something important has been violated.

In fact, the very division of priests and laity is an extension of the division of labour between those who worked within the inner sanctum of the Temple and those who were only allowed so close. The Reformation was partly an attempt to break down these divisions. As we shall see, even within this tradition the divisions are maintained, albeit in a radically revised form. But within the Catholic and Orthodox traditions, more obviously, the Temple remains the model.

It is said that when the Emperor Justinian opened the vast Hagia Sophia church in Constantinople, he declared, in a classic piece of Christian triumphalism: 'Solomon, I have surpassed you.' Sir Christopher Wren's St Paul's Cathedral continues in a similar tradition – with an influence that can be established through the lesser-known work of a Dutch rabbi, Jacob Judah Leon. In this case the Temple was not just a theoretical model for church design, but an actual one.

Judah Leon was a scholar of Sephardic descent, born in Hamburg in 1603 and raised in Holland. A translator of the Psalms and an expert in heraldry, he is better known by the adopted name Judah Leon Templo, a name given to him because of the detailed model of the Jerusalem Temple – Solomon's First Temple – that he built and took on a tour of Europe. The model was huge; in today's terms, the size of a small van. It was while this model was on display in Amsterdam that the then exiled Charles II saw it and was much impressed. Judah Leon Templo was the first Jew to receive a royal warrant and composed a special prayer for the king for use in English synagogues.

The king invited Rabbi Leon and his model to England, where it drew great crowds and was set to have a surprising influence, including on the intellectual development of the newly established Freemasonry movement. Leon Templo was probably one of the first Jewish members of a Masonic Lodge. He also came with a letter of introduction to Sir Christopher Wren, who was himself, some believe, a member of Lodge no. 2, which met close to St Paul's. Whether or not they were both Masons – a movement obsessed with the function and spiritual significance of the Temple – it was partly under Leon Templo's influence that Wren's great cathedral came to be constructed the way it was.

As we have seen, the idea of the Trinity was an extension of specifically Jewish ways of addressing the plumbing problem, but the same was also the case for church architecture. This connection was not simply a question of church architects borrowing the look of the built environment of the Temple, the link was also one of purpose: that both the Temple and the Christian church – though unlike synagogues – were intended as places of sacrifice. Within first-century Judaism the Jerusalem Temple was pretty much the only place where sacrifices were made to God. The priests of the Temple were functionaries of this sacrifice. That was their role. With the destruction of the Temple, the priestly traditions of Judaism were put into abeyance, and are only to resume if and when the Temple is rebuilt.

By contrast, the early Christians, as a consequence of recognizing the death of Jesus on the cross as itself a sacrifice – the ultimate once-and-for-all sacrifice, as the letter to the Hebrews interprets it – came to maintain the institution of the priesthood at about the same time that Jews suspended it. Here one might even argue that Christianity maintained a stronger sense of continuity with its ancient Jewish roots than what came to be the religion of the rabbis, a religion that was later refocused around the study of the Torah. While rabbinic Jews, who do not recognize Jesus as the Messiah, inevitably think of the sacrifice of the Mass as a perversion of Jewish sacrifice, built on a mistake, it was nonetheless the church and not the synagogue that set an altar at its heart. And, despite the early church's own attempts to wrestle free of its Jewish roots, it was the Church that maintained a version of the sacrificial tradition within its core purpose and so, as a consequence, much of the language of ritual purity. In other words, given the nature of the institution of the priesthood, it is unsurprising that questions of purity and impurity would continue to assert themselves within the Church – as they did at St Paul's.

Here, I believe, we reach the heart of the matter concerning Occupy. As I said, the Chapter at St Paul's never had a proper theological debate about the nature of the challenge the cathedral was facing. Had we done so, I suspect this would have been at its core. For some of my colleagues, the presence of Occupy – its very smell, its mess, its shit and urine running down Wren's famous walls – was experienced as a form of impurity that threatened the theological

156

plumbing, the effectiveness, of the cathedral as a connection between God and humanity. And here too we were replaying a disagreement that was both remarkably ancient and yet also surprisingly modern.

7.

In Act III of Shlomo Ansky's *The Dybbuk*, Leah's desperate parents send a messenger to a famous Hasidic tzaddik, or holy man, Rabbi Azriel of Miropol, who they hope will exorcize the ghostly Dybbuk from Leah's body. Azriel's grandfather was a disciple of the Baal Shem Tov, his father also a famous tzaddik. But Rabbi Azriel is too weak to succeed. 'Many generations have passed since the Temple fell,' he explains, 'and I am as many miles from the source of life, and I wither and pale ...' Instead, Azriel offers the messenger some wisdom on the nature of purity or holiness.

> RABBI AZRIEL: Which is the Holiest of lands?
> THE MESSENGER: The Holy Land.
> RABBI AZRIEL: The Holiest city?
> THE MESSENGER: Jerusalem.

The dialogue continues thus, back and forth:

> RABBI AZRIEL: The Temple in Jerusalem was the Holiest place, and the Holiest room was?
> THE MESSENGER: The Holy of Holies.
> RABBI AZRIEL: There are seventy nations, and which is the Holiest?
> THE MESSENGER: The people Israel.
> Of the twelve tribes of Israel the Holiest is Levi,

Of the Levites the Holiest are the priests,
And the Holiest of these is the High Priest of Israel.

RABBI AZRIEL: Three hundred and fifty-four are the days of the year, and which is the Holiest?

THE MESSENGER: Yom Kippur.

RABBI AZRIEL: And which is the Holiest Yom Kippur?

THE MESSENGER: When Yom Kippur falls on Shabbes.

RABBI AZRIEL: Seventy languages are spoken on earth and the Holiest is Hebrew. That Hebrew is Holiest which is found . . . ?

THE MESSENGER: In the Torah.

RABBI AZRIEL: In the Torah, which is the Holiest text?

THE MESSENGER: The Ten Commandments.

RABBI AZRIEL: And which is the Holiest word therein?

THE MESSENGER (*softly*): The Holiest word is the Shem ha-Mfoyrosh.

RABBI AZRIEL: God's own unutterable name.

Azriel pauses, and then pulls all these threads together.

RABBI AZRIEL: And this is what everyone knows: at one instant all these conjoin – on Yom Kippur on Shabbes the High Priest entered the Holy of Holies and pronounced the Shem ha-Mfoyrosh, the Tetragrammaton: Yud, Hey, Vov, Hey. At that moment of complete and utter holiness, had a single thought of sin, God forbid, a machshovve zorre, entered the mind of the High Priest, the world would have died.

This conclusion is startling, the ultimate in catastrophizing the existence of impurity within God's presence. Had the High Priest merely thought about something impure at the moment he entered the holiest of holies, the world would have exploded – like adding sodium to water. Boom.

This is the ultimate expression of the plumbing problem. The Temple is the dwelling place of God, and thus the place where God and humanity reach out to one another. But this reaching out is inherently problematic because God is holy and humanity is not: one is sacred, the other profane. And the sacred and the profane are inimical to each other – the profane being an existential threat to the sacred. Throughout the Bible any direct contact between God and humanity is deemed highly problematic. So, for instance, when Moses asks to see God directly – 'show me your Glory,' as Moses requests in Exodus 33 – he is to be disappointed: 'you cannot see my face,' God replies, 'for no one shall see me and live.' Instead of direct contact, God offers Moses the possibility of seeing his back as he glances by.

As we have seen, the Temple is a solution to the problem of how God and humanity come into contact with each other. The Temple is structured as a series of sieves, as it were, with various courtyards allowing an ever more finely graduated access. These barriers admit people closer to God depending on their respective level of holiness. With Herod's Temple, the outer balustrade marks off the whole sanctified area of the Temple precinct, on which there were signs in Latin and Greek warning Gentiles that they are not allowed to enter and that death will be the punishment for any who do. Beyond this balustrade, a series of rectangular courts allowed differentiated access.

The first court was the Court of the Women, which allowed women and men to enter, to make their sacrifices. Women, as they were considered less ritually pure than men, were not allowed to go further towards the centre. The next courtyard, the Court of the Israelites, allowed access to

Jewish men. The next was the Court of the Priests, where only the priests could enter. At the very centre was the Holy of Holies, into which, as Rabbi Azriel describes, only the High Priest could enter on one day of the year: Yom Kippur. And if the High Priest brought with him any of the impurity of the world outside, the world would end. Were the sacred and the profane to meet, it would be like some massive religious nuclear explosion. The Temple thus imagines gradations of holiness and ritual purity, allowing contact between God and humanity mediated through a series of exclusions and climaxing in the precarious and once-yearly contact between God and the High Priest.

Now it is important to emphasize that this way of understanding the relationship between God and humanity is not the only way the Hebrew Scriptures imagines this relationship to work. Many of the prophets attack the Temple as becoming an end in itself, too much about cultic sacrifice and not enough about moral virtue. 'I desire mercy, not sacrifice,' God says in Hosea. For prophets such as Hosea, sacrifice should be understood more in terms of what you give up in order to do the right thing than chopping the heads off bulls and pigeons. 'The sacrifice acceptable to God is a broken spirit; a broken and contrite heart, O God, you will not despise,' writes the Psalmist. Running counter to the theology of the priests, there is a whole tradition of Temple scepticism within prophetic Judaism – and this tradition included Jesus himself.

However, for those of a more priestly disposition, the Temple remains the pivot on which God relates to humanity. And for the priestly way of looking at things, the holy is all about separating the pure and the impure. The root of the Hebrew word for 'holy' means 'separate' – the separation of the sacred and the common or profane. Leviticus, the key text for priestly theology, expresses it thus: 'You are to distinguish between the holy and the common, and between the unclean and the clean.' Generally speaking, it is the proximity of death that constitutes the core of the unclean. Corpses are highly toxic, as are diseases like leprosy. Leakages of genital fluids – the loss of that which is generative and life-giving, as it were – constitutes ritual impurity. So, too, do leakages of blood, including menstrual blood, pus and – although there is considerable difference of interpretation here – excrement. Thus Deuteronomy 23:

> You shall have a designated area to which you shall go. With your utensils you shall have a trowel; when you relieve yourself outside, you shall dig a hole with it and then cover up your excrement. Because the Lord your God travels along with your camp to save you and to hand over your enemies to you, therefore your camp must be holy, so that he may not see anything indecent among you and turn away from you.

The separation of the holy and the profane is the separation of life and death. God is life – eternal life, pure life affirmed. And death must not be allowed to contaminate God's very nature.

8.

In *The Unbearable Lightness of Being*, the Czech novelist Milan Kundera takes a totally different view of the nature of purity, one that can be seen as the polar opposite to that expressed by Rabbi Azriel and the Jewish priestly tradition. Kundera's reflections on purity take shape in his development of the notion of kitsch as a moral problem. Typically, of course, 'kitsch' is understood as indicating poor taste, something that is overly sentimental and garish. For Kundera, however, kitsch has a far wider significance. 'Kitsch,' he proposes 'is the absolute denial of shit.' Kitsch is that let's-pretend world in which nothing unwholesome or indecent is allowed to come into view. And what is so deeply disturbing about kitsch, Kundera argues, is that it is fundamentally premised on exclusion. Kitsch casts out anything unwholesome, anything that it deems shitty or base, in order to portray a world of purity and moral decency. This could be seen as an attack on the excluding enclosures of the Temple, though Kundera does not make this connection.

When I first came across Kundera's use of the word 'kitsch', I read a newspaper story accusing a rival newspaper of air-brushing a disabled child out of a photograph they had printed of the English cricket team celebrating victory in South Africa. In the original picture the team was joined by a girl in a wheelchair. Apparently, the offending newspaper decided that her inclusion in the photo didn't fit in with the overall impression of joy and celebration they wanted to create.

Think of those Nazi propaganda films of beautiful, healthy-looking children skiing down the Bavarian Alps. 'Ahh, how lovely,' we are meant to feel. This is a world that has been puri-fied, where everything troubling has been eliminated. The logical conclusion of kitsch, argues Kundera, is the ghetto and the concentration camp – the means by which totalitar-ian regimes dispose of their shit, variously construed. As he opened the infamous exhibition of degenerate art in the summer of 1937, Hitler gave notice that 'from now on in we will wage a war of purification against the last elements of putrefaction in our culture'. For Kundera, kitsch exemplifies the aesthetics of ethnic cleansing, and he goes on to suggest that it originates in theology:

When I was small and would leaf through the Old Testament retold for children and illustrated in engravings by Gustave Doré, I saw the Lord God standing on a cloud. He was an old man with eyes, nose and a long beard and I would say to myself that if He had a mouth, He had to eat. And if He ate, He had intestines. But that thought always gave me a fright, because even though I had come from a family that was not particularly religious, I felt the idea of a divine intestine to be sacrilegious. Spontaneously, without any theological training, I, as a child, grasped the incompatibility of God and shit . . .

Later, Kundera explains that there are numerous versions of kitsch: 'Catholic, Protestant, Jewish, Communist, Fascist, democratic, feminist, European, American, National, international.' What they have in common is what he calls 'the categorical agreement with being' – the euphoric feeling of being at one with life itself. Kitsch is a sort of spurious solidarity that is established by a sentimental attachment to a cleaned-up image of humanity, the sort of image of human life that we are presented with in the first chapter of the Bible:

Behind all the European faiths, religious and political, we find the first chapter of Genesis, which tells us that the world was created properly, that human existence is good, and that we are therefore entitled to multiply. Let us call this basic faith a categorical agreement with being.

For Kundera, the deep fault at the heart of many a religious and political world view is the idea that we need to clean up humanity so that it can return to some ideal prelapsarian state of perfection. At the very centre of biblical narratives of salvation is a return to Eden, to some imagined state of at-oneness with pure being itself. And this can only take place by exclusion, by casting out that which is understood as less than perfect. For Kundera, what is less than perfect goes by the name of shit.

Kitsch offers the perfect scene, the place from which all shit, or anything apparently shit-like, has been extracted. Kitsch politics imagines beautiful blond-haired, blue-eyed children singing in perfect harmony, all handing out bunches of flowers. It imagines a Disney version of reality in which everything and everyone is perfect, wholesome, without defect. It is some crass version of a celestial heaven on earth. But the reason these kitsch images are so phenomenally dangerous is that in order to achieve this perfect scene all that is deemed not to be perfect has to be systematically eliminated. It is a world without the lame or the blind, without the ugly or distorted or the smelly. For some, it is a world without people of colour; for others a world without homosexuals. For Hitler, it was a world without Jews – hence the 'aesthetics of ethnic cleansing'. Kitsch, for Kundera, is the beautifying face of pure evil.

This is why kitsch is so deeply pernicious: in so far as real humanity is characterized by the earthiness of bodily functions, and so-called perfection is a religious and political fantasy, it turns out to be a war against humanity itself. As Kundera concludes, 'Shit is a more onerous theological problem than is evil.'

9.

As Major General Cottam was composing his words to justify the eviction of the Occupy protesters, St Paul's Cathedral was preparing for Christmas. And Christmas is the standard Christian response to the problem of kitsch.

The story of Christmas is that of God being born as a

human child in a smelly shed, surrounded by cattle. Even Jesus' parents are unsatisfactory – seemingly confused and poorly organized. From the perspective of Temple Judaism this is as offensive a story as one can possibly imagine. For what is being imagined in the Christmas narrative is a direct coming together of God and humanity, a collapse of all the walls that separate the two. God is imagined to exist precisely within the very world of dirt and sin and impurity that the priestly theologians believed it was their job to keep away from the divine. In Rabbi Azriel's story, the world is threatened with extinction if the High Priest has one impure thought in the presence of God. By contrast, in the Christian story, God is not to be distanced from 'impure' humanity. For the priestly writers, holiness means separation. Christmas, on the other hand, seeks to demolish separation, which is why, from the traditionally Jewish perspective, Christmas is the ultimate blasphemy.

The Gospel writers focus on this over and over. Jesus – the incarnation of God on earth – touches lepers and menstruating women; he constantly fraternizes with the ritually impure, with Gentiles, with drunks. He refuses to admonish his followers who fail strictly to keep the purity laws with regards to ritual washing.

Since the Middle Ages there has been a tradition in and around Barcelona of placing a statue of a defecating boy at the back of the Christmas crib scene – the so-called Caganer. Usually, the boy is squatting, with his trousers around his ankles, and a small pile of poo beneath him. People who are not used to this tradition are sometimes offended by the presence of shit so close to the birth of the baby Jesus. In this way the Caganer could be seen as the perfect representation of Christian theology – he stands for the refusal to separate the sacred from the profane, the pure from the impure. The

Caganer, like the incarnation itself, is a bomb placed underneath the book of Leviticus.

When the theologians of the first few centuries of the Christian era were struggling with the nature of the incarnation – how Jesus could be both God and human – they weren't just trying to figure out how Jesus could be made up of two very different kinds of metaphysical stuff. They were also trying to understand how the sacred and the profane were supposed to relate to each other. Many who felt the attraction of Jesus' message also believed that the collapse of this separation was going too far. Convoluted ways were sought to keep the separation in place. Christ was not really human or Christ was not really divine. Others created a firewall between the sacred and the profane within the person of Jesus himself.

Milan Kundera says that when he was a child, leafing through those Gustave Doré etchings of God and wondering about the existence of His bowels, he came to 'question the basic thesis of Christian anthropology, namely that God was created in man's image. Either/or: either man was created in God's image – and God has intestines! – or God lacks intestines and man is not like him.' Kundera references the second-century Gnostic theologian Valentinus as thinking as he did at the age of five. Jesus 'ate and drank but did not defecate', Valentinus concluded. But here Kundera's reasoning deserts him. It was precisely because of their failure to affirm that Jesus was both fully human and fully divine that Gnostics like Valentinus were officially condemned as heretics. It makes no sense to pin kitsch theology on Christianity because Christianity rejects Valentinus.

The Caganer is a reminder of a totally different theological configuration. From the perspective of official orthodox Christian doctrine, the story of Christmas is a full-scale attack on the notion of kitsch. Valentinus' theology is declared heretical precisely because it denies the full reality of the incarnation. For Valentinus, Jesus seemed human. 'Veiled in flesh the Godhead see,' as the startlingly heretical carol puts it. Orthodoxy turns out to be vastly more radical, not because it provides a way of squaring the circle of a God-man, but because it refuses to separate the divine from material reality. God is born in a stable. The divine is reimagined: not as existing in some pristine isolation, but in the shittiness of the world, all Temple boundaries collapsed.

The temptation to disassociate the divine from material reality marks the beginnings of kitsch. Once unhitched from the divine, the complexity of the world can be too easily bypassed and ignored. The orthodox formulation of the incarnation allows no way of avoiding politics, food, sex or money. Nor, as the Christian story of God goes on to make horribly clear, does it offer a way of avoiding suffering and death either.

10.

Now we have reached a very difficult place. Pause a moment. Think carefully about what is really being said here by Kundera. Kitsch is 'the aesthetics of ethnic cleansing' – it leads to the ghetto and the gulag and to the death camps. But where does kitsch come from? From theology. Kitsch – the 'denial of shit', as illustrated by Gustave Doré – is the radical disassociation of the sacred from the profane. And given the incarnation, this is much more a Jewish thing than a Christian one. So putting these two things together, Kundera comes perilously close to blaming the Jews for the murderous historical hostility they have endured. Kitsch theology is effectively racist, so Judaism is racist. He doesn't say any of this, to be fair to him. Nor, I imagine, does he even think it. Yet it is still hard to avoid this as an inevitable conclusion of his thought. And all of this has to be considered alongside those who would associate purity with purity of blood, again a familiar racist trope. These are very dark and dangerous waters, and this is partly why it matters to me so much that the purity tradition is defended.

One superficial defence goes like this. Jewish theologians do not, in fact, think of shit as being ritually impure. Nachmanides, for instance, comments on Deuteronomy's prohibition of defecating in the camp thus:

> The reason for covering excrement is not because excrement is like impurity and makes its surroundings impure . . . rather, it is forbidden to see it at the time of prayer, when the heart cleaves to the Glorious Name, because disgusting things give rise to revulsion in the soul and disrupt the concentration of the pure heart.

The problem here is that, for Kundera, what he calls shit is something more than mere faeces. It is a figure of speech for all manner of unwholesomeness. Furthermore, he does not actually care about ritual purity per se. He would, I suspect, attach the description 'kitsch' as much to Nachmanides' account of shit as to that of the Qumran and Karaite Jews for whom faeces was indeed considered a matter of ritual impurity.

No, the answer is that there is a huge misunderstanding involved in the association of Judaism with kitsch. This misunderstanding supposes that the purpose of the Temple, and of its rules and walls, is to keep God and humanity apart. But that is not it at all. The purpose of the Temple is very much opposite to this: to connect God and humanity, to establish and maintain a link between them. This is crucial. All the rules and divisions that are set up within ancient Judaism are not ways of keeping God and human beings apart; they are, as it were, more like the health-and-safety rules that are required in order to bring them together, for God and humanity to reach out to each other. In other words, the Temple theology of ancient Judaism was a way of making it clear that the interface between humanity and the divine is an extremely perilous one, not because they must remain forever separate, but precisely because they must take care how they come together.

II.

So, finally, my question is this: how does a church, or a cathedral, fail? My argument has run as follows. The role of a church, like that of the Temple – like that of Jesus, the new Temple – is to maintain a connection between God and humanity. This connection finds its original expression in creation – God's patterning of human life within the context of all that he has made. All subsequent attempts to reassert this connection refer back to this original act of creation, and the way it positioned all things within a just and proper relationship to each other. In other words, creation supplies a map of the world that has moral implications: a place for everything and everything in its place. This map is embedded within the built environment of the Temple and – in a spin-off from Judaism – within the flesh and bones of Jesus of Nazareth, both seeking to recall humanity to God's original sense of how human beings find their place in the universe.

Admittedly, I have mixed my metaphors terribly. I began with plumbing and ended up with maps. In theology, metaphors are entirely unavoidable because we can speak of God only indirectly – and only partially adequate – for exactly the same reason. Thus slippage is inevitable. In the course of this chapter we have looked at a number of different ways in which theologians have grappled with the need to connect the seemingly unconnectable. From angels to the Trinity, from philosophical analogy to the Temple – all of these theological ideas are motivated by a desire to maintain a connection with what God intended for humanity and how human beings pattern their lives according to God's plan – a word that neatly combines a sense of intention with that of cartography.

The job of religious professionals, both priests and theologians, is to help maintain the accuracy of their maps or the effective functioning of the theological plumbing that connects God and humanity. Their business is to be alert to the forces of misdirection and alienation. Words like 'purity' and 'impurity' exist in relation to this exercise. Purity is a well-functioning map. Impurity is a distorted map. This, then, is how these words have serious moral valence – and are not just a theological expression of some visceral yuck factor.

Purity, then, is a creation ordinance that describes our proper place in the world. It is a guide to how to be at one with the created order, living in accordance with the map that God has provided. These days, this way of understanding Temple purity provides a ready-made basis for an environmental theology that sets human life within the divine choreography that God has provided. The prophetic critique of the Temple is that its maps had stopped working properly because they had ceased describing the right ordering of society as God intended, an ordering that makes for the flourishing of all creation, and in particular those who are victims of economic exploitation.

12

As explored in the previous chapter, as Christianity came to define itself as separate from its Jewish parent, and as it gained power through the conversion of the Roman Empire, the relationship between (what became) Christianity and (what became) Judaism grew increasingly violent. The way Christianity came to behave towards Jews is the greatest stain on its moral credibility. And the most important thing that Christians can do is to apologize to Jews for its history of brutality and oppression towards them. That is why the 1965 papal declaration Nostra aetate was so important: it rejected the common teaching that Jews were responsible for the death of Christ. But – notwithstanding such important moves – the long history of antipathy has made it extremely difficult for both sides to recognize the depth of their connection with each other.

I return again to David Berger's objection to Chabad messianism (see Chapter 4). The core of his objection is that millions of Jews were murdered by Christians – and that any theology that positions Judaism as structurally similar to that of Christianity is profoundly offensive. It disrespects the cries of the dead.

I respect this objection even though I cannot agree with it. Christianity distinguishes itself from Judaism in two crucial respects: first, it believes the Messiah has come. Second, it articulates a relationship not just between God and his chosen people, but also between God and the whole world. These two differences certainly set Christianity and Judaism on different paths. Yet were it not for the destruction of the Temple, and the coming together of Christianity and the Roman Empire, with all the power imbalances that this created, one can imagine that Christianity would have remained a small, rather distinctive – albeit peculiar – arm of the whole rich and diverse Jewish movement: the World Service as distinct from, and playing second fiddle to, the Home Service. Did not Isaiah declare that God would gather 'all nations and tongues; and they shall come and see my glory'. Indeed, when Matthew tells the famous story of the 'three wise men' coming from the east, it is clear they weren't following some astronomical satnav – they were following the book of Isaiah, complete with its reference to gold and frankincense. Likewise, Isaiah's messianism becomes not so much a prophecy about, but the blueprint for, the Christian understanding of the Messiah's suffering and sacrificial death. Christianity is not a departure from Judaism but a very particular reading of it.

So, notwithstanding my acknowledgement of Berger's important objection, I cannot in good faith accept it. For Berger's perfectly understandable nervousness about Chabad messianism turns out to be, at base, an objection not just to those of us who find ourselves on the fault line between Christianity and Judaism, but an objection to Christianity itself.

13.

Then Jesus filled with the power of the Spirit returned to Galilee, and a report about him spread through all the surrounding country. He began to teach in their synagogues and was praised by everyone. (Luke 4: 14–15)

Having established something of the backstory, the account of Jesus' ministry as told in the New Testament can now be read as a working out of the Hebrew Scriptures. Take the version as told by Luke.

Jesus went to Nazareth, where he had been raised. On the Sabbath he went to the synagogue as he normally did and stood up to read. The synagogue assistant gave him the scroll from the prophet Isaiah. He unrolled the scroll and found the place where it was written:

> The Spirit of the Lord is upon me,
>> because he has anointed me
>> to bring good news to the poor.
> He has sent me to proclaim release to the captives
>> and recovery of sight to the blind,
>> to let the oppressed go free,
>> to proclaim the year of the Lord's favor.
>
> (Luke 4: 18–19)

He rolled up the scroll, gave it back to the synagogue assistant and sat down. Every eye in the synagogue was fixed on him. He began to explain to them, 'Today, this scripture has been fulfilled in your hearing' (Luke 4: 21).

With this passage, Jesus announces his message for the very first time. It is his declaration of intent, his manifesto. I come to bring good news to the poor, freedom for the captives, sight to the blind.

A number of things about this passage are worth noting in the context of the argument I have been developing. For although the author of the book of Luke is a Gentile, the message that Jesus proclaims here makes absolutely no sense unless understood as an expression of Jewish theology. First, and most obviously, the context is a sermon within a synagogue – the place, as the passage clearly notes, where he normally worships. But also, and crucially, the text Jesus chooses for his explosive mini-sermon is that of the prophet Isaiah.

Two features of the Isaiah passage deserve particular

attention. The first is the reference to being anointed. This is the mark of the Messiah, the mark of the new and coming king who will make Israel great again. When Jesus says that this passage has been fulfilled 'in your hearing', he is claiming the messianic mantle. The king has returned.

But this anointing, as described in the previous chapter of Luke, was highly unusual – it wasn't the kind of anointing that one would expect for a king. It didn't take place within the context of the official structures of the royal establishment, and it wasn't presided over by the High Priest. Jesus was anointed in the desert by a strange, wild man of God, John the Baptist, and he was anointed not with holy oil, but with the spirit of God. In a murky bit of the Jordan River – at the very point, as tradition would have it, that the people of Israel first crossed over to enter the Promised Land – Jesus establishes his claim.

That this was a kind of anointing is made clear by the genealogy that follows the brief description of him being baptized. This genealogy – and given the patrilineality of the time, it is a genealogy of the male line – makes it clear that Jesus is a descendant of David, but also back through David all the way to Adam, the first 'son of God'. Jesus is the new king. He is also, crucially, one who was made king – anointed – by the spirit of God that hovered over creation at the beginning of time. This is claiming a more powerful investiture than that received by David. To be anointed by the spirit is to claim kingship over the whole universe.

Luke was also the author of the book of Acts – the part 2 of his Jesus story. And, as we have already noted, this work begins with an account of what happens on the 'harvest festival' of Shavuot or Pentecost. This, too, is obviously a creation reference. Leviticus, for instance, explains the day on which it falls thus:

From the day after the Sabbath, from the day on which you bring the sheaf of the elevation offering, you shall count off seven weeks . . . You shall count until the day after the seventh Sabbath, fifty days; then you shall present an offering of new grain to the Lord.' (Leviticus 23:15)

And again, seven is code here for creation. The baptism of Jesus in the River Jordan and the baptism with fire that the disciples received at Pentecost (meaning fifty remember) are both forms of alignment with God's core purpose as expressed in creation. They are references to the map.

Here I want to continue the argument that this alignment includes a crucial element of what we would now call economic justice. And the key to understanding this aspect of creation theology is the call for a 'year of the Lord's favour', as expressed by Isaiah and echoed by Jesus in his sermon in the Nazareth synagogue. Exactly as with Shavuot, the date of this year is calculated by the author of Leviticus as creation times creation, seven times seven:

You shall count off seven weeks of years, seven times seven years, so that the period . . . gives forty-nine years . . . And you shall hallow the fiftieth year and you shall proclaim liberty throughout the land to all its inhabitants. (Leviticus 25: 8,10)

This 'year of the Lord's favour', or Jubilee year, or *shmita* (release) in Hebrew, is a description of how human beings are to imitate God's original intention and restore balance to the created order. Specifically, it seeks to restore those who had been excluded from the abundance of creation through poverty and debt. This is the Deuteronomistic take on the Jubilee:

Every seventh year you shall grant a remission of debts. And this is the manner of the remission: every creditor shall remit the claim that is held against a neighbor, not exacting it of a neighbor who is a member of the community, because the Lord's remission has been proclaimed. Of a foreigner you may exact it, but you must remit your claim on whatever any member of your community owes you. There will, however, be no one in need among you, because the Lord is sure to bless you in the land that the Lord your God is giving you as a possession to occupy, if only you will obey the Lord your God by diligently observing this entire commandment that I command you today. When the Lord your God has blessed you, as he promised you, you will lend to many nations, but you will not borrow; you will rule over many nations, but they will not rule over you. (Deuteronomy: 15: 1–6)

There is a lot to say about this passage. First, it is a way of undermining the ability of some human beings to accumulate great wealth at the expense of others. The cancelling of debt – as was called for by the movement Jubilee 2000 that had thousands of people marching for the cancellation of Third World debt by the year 2000 – was a regular and programmatic insistence on the redistribution of wealth. If debts were to be cancelled every seven, or even every fifty, years, then lending would be highly circumscribed and debt poverty eradicated. This is the release that Jesus is talking about, 'good news to the poor, freedom to the captive', in his Nazareth address. It is important to remember that the word redemption is an economic metaphor for salvation. The Jubilee redeems the poor by cancelling their debts. At Nazareth, Jesus declares that this is to be achieved in and through him.

Second, there will be huge and dark historical consequences resulting from the fact that the Jubilee provisions do not apply to foreigners and that Jews can lend to non-Jews without these debts being subject to cancellation. For those Pauline Christians who came to abandon ethnic distinctions, this proviso to the Jubilee could not apply. This is partly why Christianity came to regard all lending and charging interest on loans, to anybody, as inherently sinful. Thus when economies grew and – often for the purposes of raising an army – a government would need to borrow money, they couldn't do so from Christians, but they could from Jews. The Jews, excluded from most professions by Christian antisemitism, became extremely useful to governments as people from whom finance could be raised. Ironically, it was this passage from Deuteronomy – a passage whose principal intention was to undermine debt culture – that made it possible for Jews to become Europe's leading financiers.

As economies grew in the Middle Ages, Christians still maintained the sinfulness of lending money at interest – as indeed Islam continues to – and thus pushed Jews into performing this role. With few other options, Jews were forced into finance because Christians didn't want to be involved in it. And having opted out, Christians then blamed Jews for performing this function. Of course, this is a crucial part of the story of how Christian antisemitism, originating in the early Church and its intellectual struggle for self-definition, came to be further weaponized against Jews. Forcing Jews to perform this often unpopular function, it was easy to lay the blame for any economic misfortune on those who sought to have their loans repaid, especially when this group was an easily identifiable ethnic minority and religious 'other'.

14.

Purity, then, represents a kind of symbolic order that references God's work in creation. Creation showed how things were intended to be, and the state to which things should be returned. This symbolic order was expressed most fully in the architecture of the Jerusalem Temple – a map of the world as it should be.

This powerful symbolic order can be used for ill as well as for good. The idea that money is dirty – filthy lucre – became a way of targeting this symbolic order against the very people for whom it first spoke of God. There is little doubt, for instance, that the Occupy protest itself contained various antisemitic tropes, with references to Jewish bankers and the controlling influence of Goldman Sachs. When Jesus threw out the money-changers from the Temple, he was making the very Jewish point that creation was intended as a common treasury for all. Seen through the lens of Christian antisemitism, he was having a go at Jewish 'Shylocks'. But as well as being deeply offensive, this is a complete misunderstanding of what was going on. He wasn't criticizing the symbolic order, he was – as the prophets had done before – seeking a return to a deeper engagement with it. It was Christianity, having separated its understanding of money – and indeed the whole symbolic order – from the creation ordinance of communal flourishing, that employed the language of purity to divide the world up into the pure and impure, with Jews pushed out as dirty and unclean. This, too, was the language of the Holocaust.

Without question, the language of purity – especially when used politically, as opposed to theologically – can be extremely dangerous. Detached from the idea that 'purity regulations' offer ways of connecting up God and humanity and a symbolic representation of God's plan as expressed through creation, the very idea of purity can be used to divide people into acceptable and unacceptable, clean and dirty. Or, to put it another way, theology is a very dangerous business when you take God out of it.

6. Seven Blessings

> Jewishness, the conscious affirmation of the qualities
> that make Jews Jews, presumes a contrast between Us
> and Them. The Jews constitute an Us; all the rest of
> humanity, or, in Jewish language, the nations of the
> world, the gentiles, constitute a Them. Between Us
> and Them is a line, a boundary, drawn not in the sand
> or stone but in the mind. The line is no less real for
> being imaginary, since both Us and Them agree that
> it exists. Although there is a boundary that separates
> the two, it is crossable and not always distinct.
>
> Shaye J. D. Cohen,
> *The Beginnings of Jewishness* (1999)

I.

Operation Protective Edge was launched on 8 July 2014, yet
another crescendo in the miserable and ongoing war between
Israel and Hamas in the Gaza Strip. Over 2,000 Gazans were
killed during that seven-week conflict, and over 10,000
wounded, including nearly 3,500 children. On the other side,
sixty-seven Israeli soldiers were killed and five civilians,
including a child. I had visited Gaza ten years before, on a
trip organized by Christian Aid, and the place, and its children especially, made a lasting impression.

That first visit was made during the run-up to the Euro
2004 football final, when Greece beat Portugal. I played

football with the children in Rafah. 'Zidane, Zidane,' they lauded their hero. 'He is arabi,' they kept on reminding me. One morning they took me to see where their homes had been, close to the Egyptian border. As I stood with the children on the piles of rubble where they once had done their homework and eaten their breakfast, the Israeli army started to fire at us from the border post. With no warning, machine-gun fire pinged off the stone, kicking up dust a few yards away. Terrified, I ran behind a house to hide. The children scattered. Thank God, no one was harmed that day.

I wrote up the story of my experience of being shot at in Gaza for the *Guardian*. And so, when Protective Edge was launched, I thought it might be a good idea to return to Gaza and write another piece, maybe find some of the same children, see how their lives had developed a decade on. They would be teenagers by now and would have a very different perspective, no doubt. So I flew to Israel, hoping I could find some way into Gaza. But two days before I travelled I made an impulsive decision. I called a friend. 'I don't know if you are busy over the next few days, but I wondered if you would like to come out to Israel?' Even more impulsively, Lynn agreed.

The security desk of El Al at Heathrow was probably on extra alert, given the Gaza situation, but their line of questioning was surprisingly personal. 'What is the nature of your relationship?' the comically serious security man enquired of us as we presented our passports: Lynn's Israeli, mine British. I have learnt from bitter experience that this is absolutely not a moment for some weak attempt at humour. 'Friends,' I replied, confidently. But Lynn was less than satisfied with my answer. It is true that our relationship had been developing in a direction that suggested it was more than a friendship, but it was early stages and we hadn't even discussed it – and this didn't seem to me to be the right time to start. Lynn disagreed. 'Friends?!' she countered, quizzically. The security man was unconvinced by this apparent inconsistency and took her off for further interrogation.

Lynn and I got married on a warm February evening in 2016 in the beautiful port city of Jaffa, in a large stone house overlooking the sea. Fifty miles up the coast from Gaza, Jaffa feels like another world. These days it has become a gentrified suburb of Tel Aviv – an ancient Arab town being gobbled up by Israeli yuppies looking for old-world charm and 'authentic' hummus. Tel Aviv is just over a century old; Jaffa is 4,000 years old. It was through this ancient port that the prophet Jonah fled from God's call to him to go and preach to the dangerous people of Nineveh. It was through here that magnificent Lebanese cedar trees were brought ashore for the construction of both the first and the second Temples. And it was here, according to the book of Acts, that Peter had a vision that led to the repeal of historic Jewish dietary laws: all foods, being made by God, were then to be considered clean and good enough to eat. Here, as Acts explains, Gentiles were first considered to be among the people of the God of Israel: 'Then God has given even to Gentiles the repentance that leads to life.'

The house belonged to a friend of my mother-in-law, Limor Tiroche, a food writer for the Israeli newspaper *Haaretz*, and a fabulous cook. We had little lamb and chickpea dumplings with a lemon tahini dressing, filo pastry parcels with spinach and sumach, wonderful little pittas with roasted cauliflower and massabha. The wine came from the Red Boat vineyard in my new father-in-law's village, Karmei Yosef, up in the foot-hills of the Jerusalem forest. It was just perfect.

The service was conducted in the hallway of the house. The chuppah was unfurled and we stood beneath it, with friends and family gathered before us. I had learned my lines in Hebrew and stuttered out the traditional form of commitment. Seven blessings were pronounced. The glass was stamped on and the congregation shouted their approval. I cried, of course.

But it wasn't a proper wedding – at least, it had no official status. There is no provision in Israeli law for a non-Jew like me to marry a Jew within Israel. Indeed, there is no provision for many couples to marry there. That's why the fifty-minute flight from Tel Aviv to Larnaca in Cyprus is regularly full of loved-up couples. They get off the flight, do the paperwork in Cyprus, have a quick drink, then catch the next plane home, all in the same day. Either because one of the partners is an atheist, or because one of them is not considered sufficiently Jewish by Israel's Chief Rabbinate, there is no marriage option available to them in Israel. It's a crazy system that highlights the dominance of the Israeli state's restrictions on who counts as Jewish.

That's why the officiant at our wedding was not acting in an official capacity. As it happened, we had officially married in a Register Office in Mayfair a couple of days before flying out to Tel Aviv. Still, a few years later, Lynn applied for an Israeli passport for our children, the embassy official refused to acknowledge that we were properly married. Of course the children could have an Israeli passport, they explained, but they just couldn't use their father's surname – their surname – on it. In a rather feisty exchange, Mrs Fraser told them where they could stick their passports.

2.

The complexity of Jews marrying non-Jews has a long and difficult backstory going back for millennia. Upstairs in the British Museum, carefully protected behind special glass and watched over by CCTV, there is a small broken pottery cylinder – a bit like a flattened-out rugby ball. Discovered during an archaeological dig in 1879, and dating back to the sixth century BCE, this undistinguished-looking object is the so-called Cyrus Cylinder and written on its surface is one of the most fascinating texts of the ancient world. Some have described it as the world's first charter of human rights.

Cyrus was 'the king of the universe', as the cylinder lauds him. Originally the king of Persia, in 539 BC Cyrus conquered his enemies, the Babylonians. The Cylinder lays out a very different approach that Cyrus took to slaves within his new empire: they were free to leave and to re-establish the temples to their gods. As the cylinder puts it, 'the gods who dwelt there I returned to their home and let them move into an eternal dwelling. All their people I collected and brought them back to their homes.' This meant that, among other conquered peoples, the Babylonian Jews could return home and were free to rebuild their Temple. The book of Isaiah addresses the Persian king in the most exulted terms possible: 'to his messiah, to Cyrus, whom I [YHWH or Yahweh] took by his right hand to subdue nations before him.' The idea that a Persian king might be described in the Hebrew Scriptures as the Messiah is quite remarkable – but this fits with the whole idea that the Messiah was the one who would make Israel great again, the central belief of messianic expectation. To Jewish exiles, Cyrus was the great liberator.

Jews returned to their historic homeland in stages, led by the prophets Nehemiah and Ezra. Their hopes were high and their excitement understandable, but when the prophet Ezra led his people back from Babylon to Jerusalem – the Bible says 42,360 of them, plus servants and singers – what they discovered wasn't exactly the place that their parents and grandparents had so lovingly described. Decades of exile had nourished a complex and distorted nostalgia for the city of David and Solomon. 'By the rivers of Babylon we sat down and wept, when we remembered Zion,' sang the Psalmist, wistfully. Much effort had been made to keep the idea of Zion alive in their mind's eye, but after seventy years of exile what they actually remembered was as much a thing of the imagination as of reality. Or, to put it another way, the period of exile had been richly creative, with many scholars believing that this was the period when much of what we now know as the Hebrew Bible began to be written down and compiled.

This makes sense. A group of people, exiled from their homeland and keen to maintain their collective identity, might well have felt the need to write down the stories of their past as a way of protecting what it was that made them different. Just as, centuries later, the first rabbis sought to protect their common identity after the destruction of the Second Temple by writing down and codifying the oral law, so too, after the destruction of the First Temple, the people of Israel had used the written word as something to gather around – to remind them who they were. In fact, this task of reimagining who they were as a people was to prove the first and decisive step in the transformation of a geographical identity – now temporarily lost – into a religious/cultural one: Judaeans began their transformation into Jews.

Captivity in Babylon hadn't been slavery in the same sense that the Pharaohs had enslaved Moses' generation long before. Unlike the Egyptians, the Babylonians didn't capture a defeated people in order to work them to death on grandiose building projects. Forced deportation was simply the way the Babylonians organized their empire – it was a vast human resources project, recycling the cream of human talent within their conquered territories through what was effectively a great labour exchange located in their capital city. They didn't simply seek to requisition an army of manual labour – though there was clearly some of that – but also aimed to recondition former enemies into loyal Babylonian citizens. Indeed, many in the Jewish diaspora had been employed in the upper echelons of Babylonian society. This allowed a kind of Jewish intelligentsia to develop. And what they wrote about was home – camp-fire stories, as it were, told to remind each other who they were and where they had come from.

But the Judea that they so fondly remembered had disappeared long ago. Back in 587 BCE the Babylonian king Nebuchadnezzar, and his strong-man army commander Nebuzaradan, had wiped it from the face of the earth. The people of Jerusalem had picked the wrong side in the global power politics between the great empires of Babylon and Egypt – and they were quashed. Solomon's glorious Temple was completely destroyed, along with the whole social and religious infrastructure that it had sustained:

> In the fifth month, on the seventh day of the month – which was the nineteenth year of King Nebuchadnezzar, king of Babylon – Nebuzaradan, the captain of the bodyguard, a servant of the king of Babylon, came to Jerusalem. He burned the house of the Lord, the king's house, and all the houses of Jerusalem; every great house he burned down. All the army of the Chaldeans who were with the captain of the guard broke down the walls around Jerusalem. Nebuzaradan the captain of the guard carried into exile the rest of the people who were left in the city and the deserters who had defected to the king of Babylon – all the rest of the population. But the captain of the guard left some of the poorest people of the land to be vinedressers and tillers of the soil. (2 Kings 25: 8–12)

Little is known about these 'poorest people' who were left behind in Jerusalem when the brightest were deported off to Babylon. But with their economy and infrastructure having been thoroughly destroyed by the Babylonians, they didn't have anything like the resources to rebuild what had gone before – and certainly not to re-create the glory of Solomon's famous Temple. A number of these people of the land were from Samaria, and came to be known as Samaritans. The Samaritans established their own cult on Mount Gerazim above the city of Shechem, now known as Nablus. They continued to maintain that their religious practices had more in common with the religion that existed in Israel before the Babylonian captivity, and that Gerazim, not Jerusalem, was the proper place for the Temple. This increasingly bitter division between the religion of the people of the land and that of the returning exiles partly explains how Samaritans became 'representative outsiders' in the eyes of those who looked to Jerusalem as the location of the true Temple. The New Testament story of the 'Good Samaritan' is supposed to be shocking because Samaritans had long been held up as the enemy within and thus unworthy of any moral commendation.

Unsurprisingly, therefore, the returning exiles found they had much less in common with those who had remained in and around Jerusalem. In Babylon, their ideas had changed over the generations; the Judaean exiles had come into contact with a culture even older than their own. And this culture had facilitated the writing of much of the Bible. Indeed, only relatively recently has the extent of the influence of Babylonian culture on the authors of the Bible begun to be fully appreciated.

Here is one example. In 1844, a young English explorer discovered the ruins of the lost city of Nineveh on the outskirts of modern-day Mosul. The most intriguing part of the find was a library of strange clay tablets. No one could read their spiky markings and they were shipped back to the British Museum for scholars to work on. It was decades later, in 1872, that an amateur enthusiast, George Smith, made an astonishing discovery as he was learning to translate the cuneiform script. Working on a mid-seventh century BC tablet, he began to read a story that sounded a lot like one he had learned in Sunday school. The god Ea warned Utnapishtim about a coming flood and told him to build a large boat. He was to fill the boat with 'all the beasts and animals of the field'. The flood lasted six days and nights, after which the boat came to rest on the top of a mountain. Utnapishtim then sent out a dove, a swallow and a raven to find dry land. Smith suddenly realized he was reading a version of Noah's ark, and apparently he was so excited by this discovery that he took his clothes off and ran naked around the museum.

Smith was right to be excited. The story of the flood in the Epic of Gilgamesh long pre-dates the writing of the Bible, and the Genesis account is clearly influenced by it. This probably means that the book of Genesis as we know it is an exilic or post-exilic, but exile-influenced phenomenon. Professor Walter Brueggemann goes further in his book *The Prophetic Imagination*: 'the Old Testament in its final form is a product of and a response to the Babylonian exile.' In other words, the Old Testament is refugee literature. The stories may or may not go back centuries; some may have been historical, some mythological, some a combination of the two – many scholars dispute the historicity of the exodus, for example – but whatever their origins, these narratives were being compiled and edited and reworked by people traumatized by the experience of exile and the threat it posed to their identity. It was here, hundreds of miles from home, among exiles from many other lands, and with Babylon's famous ziggurat reaching up into the sky, that the story of the tower of Babel was written down. It was from within this confusing multicultural mash-up that the Judaeans would work hard to hold on to their own sense of who they were.

This is also the heart of the story of the book of Daniel, which is all about maintaining one's identity amid powerful pressures to conform to the dominant culture. The book begins with Daniel's deportation from Jerusalem by Nebuchadnezzar. Talent-spotted by the Babylon court, he was employed in the royal civil service where he was taught the native language and its literature. But despite the pressure to assimilate, he continued his prayers to the God of Israel, even when such prayers are banned. And as punishment for his refusal to cease praying he was famously thrown into the lion's den. God, of course, saved him. The moral of the story is clear: whatever the pressure to conform to the surrounding culture, one must maintain one's identity, even under the threat of death. When there is a Temple to worship in, the Temple itself establishes a stable identity for those who worship. But when the Temple is destroyed, the question of who counts as 'one of us' is raised to new and critical levels. The sociologist Fredrik Barth called it 'boundary maintenance'.

Interestingly, most exiles did not follow the prophets Ezra and Nehemiah back to the homeland and chose to stay in Babylon – and that itself says something about the relatively benign conditions that operated for those Babylonian captives. It is also why the Jewish community in Baghdad is among the oldest in the world. It was here that the Babylonian Talmud was compiled and that Jewish learning thrived. When Jerusalem fell again, this time to the Romans, it was Baghdad that became the centre of Jewish life for over a thousand years. Now, tragically, only a handful of Jewish families remain. More recent conditions were not as accommodating as they were under Cyrus. Between 1950 and 1952, some 130,000 members of the Iraqi Jewish community were airlifted to the State of Israel. Significantly, the code name for this relocation was Operation Ezra and Nehemiah.

Those who followed the original Ezra and Nehemiah and other leaders of the community back to Judaea brought with them all the existential anxieties about boundary maintenance from seventy years of exile. And they were disappointed that their homeland didn't live up to their expectations. Among other things, those who had remained in the land – Samaritans and others – had not felt the need to maintain the strict boundaries of their community, and many had married foreign women. Ezra, chapter 9, memorably describes Ezra's reaction on finding this out.

> After these things had been done, the officials approached me and said, 'The people of Israel, the priests, and the Levites have not separated themselves from the peoples of the lands with their abominations, from the Canaanites, the Hittites, the Perizzites, the Jebusites, the Ammonites, the Moabites, the Egyptians, and the Amorites. For they have taken some of their daughters as wives for themselves and for their sons. Thus the holy seed has mixed itself with the peoples of the lands, and in this faithlessness the officials and leaders have led the way.' When I heard this, I tore my garment and my mantle, and pulled hair from my head and beard, and sat appalled.

The book of Ezra ends with a long list of names and then the sentence: 'All these had married foreign women, and they sent them away with their children.' Ezra says nothing about Jewish women marrying non-Jewish men. Nor does he say how the women and their children survived being cast out of the community – he was apparently unconcerned. Ezra had one interest only: the holy race must not be mingled with the impurity of the goyim. Purity must be maintained.

3.

The idea that God's chosen people should not marry outsiders was not, of itself, an entirely novel invention. That idea was first established by Deuteronomy:

> When the Lord your God brings you into the land that you are about to enter and occupy, and he clears away many nations before you—the Hittites, the Girgashites, the Amorites, the Canaanites, the Perizzites, the Hivites, and the Jebusites, seven nations mightier and more numerous than you – and when the Lord your God gives them over to you and you defeat them, then you must utterly destroy them. Make no covenant with them and show them no mercy. Do not intermarry with them, giving your daughters to their sons or taking their daughters for your sons, for that would turn away your children from following me, to serve other gods. Then the anger of the Lord would be kindled against you, and he would destroy you quickly. But this is how you must deal with them: break down their altars, smash their pillars, hew down their sacred poles, and burn their idols with fire. For you are a people holy to the Lord your God; the Lord your God has chosen you out of all the peoples on earth to be his people, his treasured possession. (Deuteronomy 7:1–6)

What is important to note about this passage is that it is very specific about the sort of people that God's chosen people were not to marry: their enemies. There is no prohibition here against Jews marrying foreigners per se. The list of those to whom marriage was denied was a list of those with whom the Jews had been at war.

In many parts of the Hebrew Bible, Jews marry non-Jews – including those proscribed by Deuteronomy. The list is a considerable and distinguished one. Judah married an Ethiopian. Joseph married an Egyptian. Moses married a Moabite and an Egyptian. David – whose great-grandmother was Ruth, a Moabite – married a Philistine. And the great King Solomon married just about anyone he could get his hands on – 700 wives and 300 concubines, including Pharaoh's daughter and women from Moab, Ammon, Edom, Sidon, and the Hittites. Later, a number of authors of the Bible, especially those of the 'make Israel great again' movement, would pinpoint Solomon's taking of foreign wives as the moment when the fortunes of Israel took a decisive turn for the worse; this was the beginning of the end of the golden era of the kings of Israel. But comment on the excesses of Solomon's later reign aside, intermarriage between Jews and non-Jews often passed without comment.

With Ezra, all this would change. The ban on intermarriage became universal, and the experience of exile was at the root of the change. As Shaye Cohen explains in *The Beginnings of Jewishness*:

> Biblical Israel was a nation living on its own land and had no need for a general prohibition of intermarriage with all outsiders. Attitudes changed when conditions changed. In the wake of the destruction of the temple in 587 BCE, Judaea lost any semblance of political independence, the tribal structure of society was shattered, and the Israelites were scattered among the nations. In these new circumstances marriage with outsiders came to be seen as a threat to Judaean (Jewish) identity and was widely condemned.

Extending Deuteronomy, Ezra developed a novel theology of Israel as a holy seed – or holy race. In his 1942 book *Marriage Laws in the Bible and the Talmud*, Rabbi Louis Epstein describes this as the invention of a racial ideology concerned with purity of blood – though in actual fact blood is never mentioned. Rather, what is invented here is the need for a pure genealogy, one uncorrupted by biological descent from foreigners. Strictly speaking, something similar was already required of priests, or perhaps just of the high priest. According to the book of Leviticus, the high priest had to maintain his genealogical purity by marrying only a virgin who was herself descended from the priestly cast – 'a virgin of his own kin' (Leviticus 21:14). It is possible that Ezra took this principle and extended it to all Jews. And with this move the idea that the Jewish people existed as a genealogical category – as distinct from simply being people who came from the land of Judah – was born. For some writers, the transgression of this boundary became a capital crime. The book of Jubilees takes an extreme position:

> And if there is any man who wishes in Israel to give his daughter or his sister to any man who is of the seed of the Gentiles he shall surely die, and they shall stone him with stones, for he has wrought shame in Israel; and they shall burn the woman with fire, because she has dishonoured the house of her father, and she shall be rooted out of Israel.

But the Ezra/Jubilees attitude towards intermarriage was not to be the last word on the subject. Far from it. The rabbis of the first few centuries BCE disagreed with Ezra, certainly with the book of Jubilees and with each other, as to the reasons for a ban on intermarriage and the extent of this ban. Indeed, the majority position in both the Palestinian and Babylonian traditions of the Talmud tended to revert back to the more limited Deuteronomistic line. The rabbis were clearly exercised by the issue of mixed marriages, but did not follow Ezra's position that mixed marriages, and the children they produced, were a violation of the holy seed. Generally, they saw the problem more as a moral/religious one – that foreigners would lead the people of Israel away from the worship of the one true God – rather than a genealogical one. After all, conversion to the religion of the Jews was acceptable in certain circumstances – as it hadn't been to the author of the book of Jubilees. As Christine Hayes, Professor of Religious Studies in Classical Judaica at Yale University, puts it, 'conversion has the power to reclassify foreign seed as native seed'. So with the rabbis the strict impermeability of the boundary between Jews and non-Jews that had been established by Ezra was partially reversed.

There is an argument to say that it was Pauline Christianity that made much more of Ezra's 'holy seed' position than did the early rabbis themselves. Paul, of course, was a Pharisee before his conversion, and the basic theological position of the Pharisees was that priestly rules of behaviour should be democratized and extended to lay people as well as to priests. This meant that Paul may well have been inherently sympathetic to the way in which Ezra took the rules for priests as found in the book of Leviticus and extended them universally. This is speculation on my part, but what seems clear is that Paul adapted Ezra when he spoke of believers and unbelievers not being yoked together because this connection would defile the holy body of the believer, which is the dwelling place of the spirit. For Paul, mixed marriages linked the holy and the profane, thereby contaminating Christ with the impurity of unbelief. For him, it was not seeds but bodies that must be kept pure. These are different categories, of course, but not unconnected. For later

Christian writers, intermarriage between a believer and an unbeliever was banned because the believer must maintain their moral purity. Temple language of pure and impure was extended to the new Temple: the people of God, the body of Christ. And the most basic existential threat to the living stones of this new Temple came to be seen as sexual: bodily co-mingling.

4.

Just as Christians sought to distance themselves from Jews, so Jews also tried to keep themselves apart from Christians. Second-century Jewish texts, primarily those included in a collection of supplementary material to the Mishnah, the Tosefta for example (a compilation of Jewish oral law), contain a number of such passages. One text advises that if the Torah scrolls of Jewish Christians are on fire, 'proper' Jews are forbidden from saving them from the fire, even though they contain the divine name: 'R. Tarfon said: I swear by the lives of my children that if these scrolls were to come into my hands, I would burn them and their divine names.' The parchment sheets of the Jewish Christian Torah scrolls are referred to as *ha-gilyonim*, which sounds a little like a pun on the Greek-language Christian name for the Gospels, *euangelion*.

In many of these writings Jesus is referred to as Yeshu ben Panthera, which is a deliberate insult against the paternity of Jesus. As a counter to the Christian story of Jesus' miraculous birth from the Virgin Mary, rabbinic Jews reframed the story so that Jesus was the issue of an adulterous relationship between Mary and a Roman soldier called Panthera. In other words, Jesus was a bastard. This, then, became one of the standard insults that Jews would direct at Christians through-out the Middle Ages. Here is an example from the Tosefta:

> It once happened that R. Eleazar b. Damah was bitten by a snake, and Jacob of Kfar Sama came to heal him in the name of Yeshua b. Penitra.

But despite the fact that Rabbi Eleazar was understanda-bly keen to be healed, and wanted to supply biblical evidence to the rabbinic authorities that this was indeed acceptable, he died before he was able to make his case. 'Fortunate are you, Ben Damah, for you have expired in peace and did not breach the fence,' was Rabbi Yishmael's reaction. Better to die than to receive healing from a Christian, as a fence now exists separating the two. And this fence must never be crossed in any circumstances.

Another, similar story tells of the arrest of Rabbi Eleazar for once having had a conversation with a Jewish Christian. Later, the rabbi confesses his fault. 'I was strolling down the main street in Sepphoris [a small village a few miles north of Nazareth] when I met Jacob of Kfar Sikhnin, who told me a matter . . . in the name of Yeshua b. Pantira, and it pleased me.' The arrest brought Rabbi Eleazar to his senses. 'I trans-gressed the words of the Torah,' he admits, 'One should always flee from what is ugly and from whatever appears to be ugly.' These stories, traditionally dated from around the beginning of the second century, tell of the increasing hos-tility between the rabbinic version of Judaism – soon to be the official version – and the Jewish Christian community, who were now being attacked from both sides.

At some point, this anti-Christian polemic came to be established within the Jewish service of daily prayer in the notorious Birkat ha-minim blessing. Admittedly with signif-icant discrepancies between the two accounts, nonetheless both the Jerusalem and Babylonian versions of the Talmud locate the introduction of this divisive bit of liturgy to the Council of Yavneh, soon after the destruction of the Second Temple. As mentioned earlier, others have disputed this dating, even the existence of the council itself. Was it a later Jewish attempt to retro-fit early rabbinic Judaism with something similar to the Christian Council of Nicaea? asks Daniel Boyarin. What Boyarin has in mind here is that the formation of a centralizing rabbinic authority was borrowed from the developing Christian idea of orthodoxy, both shadowing each other, just as they vigorously repudiated each other in a kind of mimetic denial.

Irrespective of whether this is right or not, by the fourth century, when official Roman Christianity was legalizing its separation from Jews, the synagogue came to understand the Birkat ha-minim as a specifically anti-Christian prayer, a curse on Christians. Certainly from the fourth century onwards, Jewish Christians were disowned by both the now well-established Jewish and Christian orthodoxies. And in the West at least, the original religion of Jesus of Nazareth was being squeezed out of existence.

It is way beyond the scope of my concern to provide anything like a comprehensive history of the boundary maintenance issues that exist between Christians and Jews. As we have seen with David Berger's reaction to the Lubavitcher Rebbe, the history of forced conversions and the violence of anti-Jewish persecution by Christians throughout the Middle Ages and on to the Holocaust, is a powerful and entirely understandable reason for Jews to resist any muddying of these boundaries. Even so, it remains the case that the ways in which boundary maintenance is understood has changed according to circumstance. And no change was as significant as the establishment of the State of Israel in 1947. At this point a new and very different authority to that of the rabbis came to the fore. Just as the early rabbis accepted that 'conversion [to Judaism] has the power to reclassify foreign seed as native seed', with the establishment of Israel another side to this question came into sharper focus: namely, whether conversion of Jews to Christianity had the power to reclassify native seed as foreign. With the establishment of the State of Israel, and the need for this new state to have its own immigration policy, the question of who was and who was not a Jew took another turn.

5.

Luckily for Oswald Rufeisen his name sounded more German than Jewish. Born in Poland, yet close to the Austrian border, the young Oswald grew up speaking German at school as well as Polish. Later in life he would converse fluently in eight languages. It was this gift for language that enabled him to hide his Jewishness and undoubtedly saved his life.

Oswald's brother, Arieh, left for Palestine in 1941, just before the outbreak of war, but Oswald didn't manage to secure a visa. At the age of seventeen, he was swept up in the violence and chaos of the Nazi invasion. Separated from his parents, arrested and imprisoned, Oswald escaped the German death squads at first by being a useful shoemaker, and then, after escaping captivity, by passing himself off as a non-Jewish Pole. He was constantly terrified of exposure, but hid in plain sight, securing a job with the police as a translator. It was in the police offices that Oswald first learnt of the Nazi plans to liquidate the Mir ghetto. He passed on a warning to the ghetto leadership – knowing that it was extremely risky to do so – and helped them to lay their hands on weapons. As a result some 200 Jews were able to escape into the forest. A few days later, 560 of Mir's Jews were murdered by the SS. But in saving others, Oswald himself was exposed, and again he was on the run, sleeping rough, hiding in barns and wheat fields.

Finally Oswald sought sanctuary in the local convent, run by the Order of the Sisters of the Resurrection. Attending church on Sunday with the sisters, Oswald was overwhelmed by the Gospel story the local priest told about the Good Samaritan, a story in which a helpless Jew is attacked by robbers and left for dead. Ignored by a passing priest and Levite, the Jew was finally helped by one of the hated Samaritans, who stopped and tended to the man's wounds and paid a local innkeeper to look after him. 'Go and do likewise,' is Jesus' instruction at the end of the story. Though the nuns were worried about harbouring someone who was being hunted by the Nazis, the Mother Superior was convinced that this story was speaking to them directly about the need to protect Oswald.

This sermon also had a profound effect on Oswald himself. In the book of his testimony, as told to Nechama Tec, *In the Lion's Den: The Life of Oswald Rufeisen*, he would describe it as marking the beginning of his conversion to Christianity.

In the convent, all alone, among strangers, I created an artificial world for myself. I pretended that the 2000 years had never happened. In this make-believe world of mine, I am confronted by Jesus of Nazareth. . . . You must realize that not all history about Jesus is the history of the church. The history of Jesus is a fragment of Jewish history. . . . Suddenly, and I don't know how, I identify his suffering and resurrection with the suffering of my people and the hope of their resurrection. I begin to think that if a man who is just and pure dies, not for his sins but because of circumstance, there must be a God, because it is God who brings him back to life. Then I think that if there is justice toward Christ in the form of resurrection there will be some kind of justice toward my people too. . . . In the end my move to Christianity was not an escape from Judaism but, on the contrary, a way of finding answers to my problems as a Jew.

Oswald was baptized in the convent, and later became a priest and a monk, taking the new name of Daniel – a reference to him having escaped from the lion's den of the Nazi death-squads.

After the war, keen to be reunited with his brother and, as a lifelong Zionist, also wanting to live among those Oswald regarded as 'his people', the now Fr Daniel left Europe for Palestine. He disembarked at Haifa wearing the brown habit of a Carmelite monk, with a cross around his neck. His brother Arieh greeted him off the boat, full of emotion at their reunion, but confused and embarrassed by his choice of clothing. Like others, he experienced his brother's conversion as a betrayal and a tragedy. A number of Mir's Jews – those Oswald had helped to escape and who had made their way to Israel – came to see him, delighted to be able to thank him for his courage in the war, but distressed at his conversion to Christianity. It was a common reaction: in becoming Daniel, Oswald had forfeited his right to be thought of as a Jew.

What confused Daniel's friends also perturbed the Israeli authorities. On his application form for Israeli nationality Daniel put down 'Jew' under ethnicity and 'Roman Catholic' under religion. According to the Israeli Law of Return (1950), any Jew who chose to settle in Israel had a right to automatic citizenship. But was Daniel a Jew? The immigration authorities first refused to allow him to put 'Jew' in his passport. Fr Daniel took them to court. It was a question that would eventually have to be decided by the Supreme Court of Israel in a landmark ruling.

The problem faced by the court was this. In terms of Halakha (rabbinic religious law), there is no question that Daniel was a Jew. A Jew is someone born of a Jewish mother. A Jew who does not follow the law is still a Jew. An atheist Jew is a Jew. A Jew who denies being a Jew is still a Jew. Even a Christian Jew is still a Jew – a heretic, of course, and, for many, to be despised. But once a Jew, always a Jew.

The other problem was this. The state of Israel was established, and gained its moral justification, as a lifeboat for the Jewish people, a sanctuary within their historic homeland for those who have experienced persecution since their expulsion from Jerusalem in the first century AD. After the Holocaust, the need for a place of safety, a state for the Jewish people, was given renewed impetus and international support. If you were Jewish enough for the gas chambers, you were Jewish enough for Israeli nationality.

Nechama Tec's book relates how the presiding judge, Moshe Silberg, expressed the dilemma of the judges:

> the great psychological difficulty that we encounter from the beginning of this very unusual trial is ... as Jews we owe to Oswald Rufeisen our deepest thanks ... We see before us a man who in the darkest years of the Holocaust, in Europe, endangered his life many times, countless times, for his Jewish brothers and carried out activities of rescue that were as brave and courageous as literally throwing himself into a lion's den against the Nazis. How can we deny such a person his deepest quest in life to completely fuse with the people that he loves and to become a citizen?

Nonetheless, in December 1962, the Supreme Court of Israel rejected Daniel's claim to be admitted to Israel under the Jewish Right of Return with a majority verdict. Officially at least, in becoming a Christian, Daniel had stopped being a Jew.

There is a real theological irony here. During the period that the Bible was being written, being a Jew was a matter of ethnicity and commitment to place. It was only because the early Church, under Paul's influence, came to think of religion as a matter of belief that the idea developed that what you believe is the defining feature of religiosity. And as Daniel Boyarin has powerfully argued, the idea that Judaism is itself a set of beliefs is a very late development, perhaps even an eighteenth-century one. Moreover, this idea that Judaism is fundamentally about belief is a very Christian-sounding proposition. Yet the Israeli Supreme Court decided to reject Fr Daniel's application on the grounds of his belief system and irrespective of his ethnicity and his commitment to place. In other words, they made a decision by applying a very Pauline idea of how faith and ethnicity/place are related. Daniel, they argued, was too Christian for Israel. Arguably, it was the court that was reasoning most like a Christian.

Of the five judges who made the decision, the one dissenting voice came from Judge Haim Cohn: 'If the plaintiff's religion was not Christianity nobody would have doubted his Jewishness,' he claimed. And about this he was surely correct. Israel's first Prime Minister, David Ben-Gurion, had a fascination with Buddhism – albeit probably not to the extent that one could describe him as a Buddhist. Nonetheless, lots of Jews are Buddhists, and many find this unproblematic. Indeed, Jewish-Buddhist can be hyphenated without alarm in a way that Jewish-Christian cannot.

Judge Cohn was clearly much affected by the Brother Daniel

judgement. Two years later, in 1966, Cohn delivered the annual Moshe Smoira Memorial Lecture at the Hebrew University of Jerusalem. In it he presented the view that the trial of Jesus was a Roman stitch-up. In a follow-up full-length book on the subject, Cohn carefully unpicked the view that the Jews were responsible for the death of Christ. Cohn himself was an orthodox Jew. He studied under the famous Rabbi Abraham Isaac Kook at the Mercaz HaRav yeshiva in Jerusalem and became a cantor within the ultra-orthodox community of Mea Shearim. In other words, pretty *frum* – yet he was still able to conclude his powerful account of the trial of Jesus with these words:

> Hundreds of generations of Jews . . . have . . . been made to suffer all manner of torment, persecution, and degradation for the alleged part of their forefathers in the trial and crucifixion of Jesus, when, in solemn truth, their forefathers took no part in them but did all that they possibly and humanly could to save Jesus, whom they dearly loved and cherished as one of their own, from his tragic end at the hands of the Roman oppressor.

6.

To say that the Jews are God's chosen people is to say that there are others who are not. Or, at least – and this is an important qualification – that they are not chosen by God for the same purpose.

This qualification is often missed. And there are many who object to the perceived exclusivity of the idea of being chosen on the grounds this claim gives Jews a sense of entitlement and that this entitlement has dangerous political ramifications, not least, currently, for Palestinians. Scholar

of the Old Testament Walter Brueggemann writes: 'Chosenness issues in entitlement, exclusion and extraction. From
that it follows that chosenness characteristically issues in
violence.'

As we have seen, adherents of Pauline Christianity object
to the ethnic exceptionalism implied by the term 'chosen
people' and designate the Church – based on belief rather
than ethnicity – as the legitimate bearer of God's chosenness. This move makes chosenness ethnically neutral and so
apparently more inclusive, but nonetheless it limits it to those
who have accepted Jesus and the true Messiah. Thus, for
instance, the words of the hymn:

> Ye chosen seed of Israel's race,
> Ye ransomed of the fall,
> Hail Him who saves you by His grace,
> And crown Him Lord of all.

What looks like a universal here is actually just
another form of exclusion: Christians 'in'; all others 'out'.
In other words, the Church takes Jewish exceptionalism
and re-tools it as Christian exceptionalism. There is still an
'us' and 'them' – it is just that the boundaries are redefined.
Indeed, for Brueggemann there is an unbroken line of suc-
cession from the Jewish exceptionalism of the Old
Testament to the 'Make America Great Again' exceptionalism of Donald Trump. He writes:

> This chosenness – in the cases of Israel, the church, the
> United States and white hegemony – takes on an ideological
> force that is unquestioned in its legitimacy and, for the most
> part, unrestrained in its practice. Chosenness is simply taken
> for granted with a kind of self-satisfied innocence that
> refuses any self-critical awareness.

I profoundly disagree with Brueggemann here – because there is something else to chosenness that he fails to acknowledge. Chosenness is also about belonging, about being counted among some treasured 'us'. And this cannot – must not – be discounted. Brueggemann's progressive politics blinds him to this basic human need.

At the beginning of this book, I described a plan that I made to try and write my way back to happiness – or, at least, to write my way out of misery. When I made that plan, it was little more than a hunch that words have healing power. I conjectured that the amount of time it would take to write this book would see me through the period of unhappiness that I was going through. I had no idea what the process would involve, what would be discovered along the way, or how long it would take. Words can come quickly. Healing takes time. The other thing I could not have estimated was how successful the book was going to be in these terms. And, extraordinary though it may seem, it was a discussion about the book's title that was probably the breakthrough moment.

It is 2017. My mother-in-law, Vered, has come over from Israel to see Louie, her new grandchild. She has good English, but not perfect. And one evening she asks me to try and explain what my book is all about. I try my best. 'And what is the title?' she asks. Now, from the moment the book was pitched to the publishers, the title was 'Not Chosen'. It was a book about not being Jewish, being a Christian priest with a non-Jewish mother – so, obviously, I'm not Jewish. But my father is, my wife is, and so is our new baby. There is a brokenness about my family history that a strange encounter with an oil painting in a Liverpool synagogue forced into the open.

After trying to explain all this, my mother-in-law offered her considered opinion. She was blunt in the way Israelis often are: 'Wrong title', she said. As a pretty secular-minded Jew, she didn't care too much for the theological contortions that I offered about the complex relationship between Christianity and Judaism. And with the insouciance of the insider, neither did she really bother too much with the whole question of who is and who isn't Jewish. Born in Jerusalem, Vered was married to the film director Assi Dayan, troubled son of the famous Israeli general and defence minister, Moshe Dayan. That's like being married into the Israeli Kennedys.

No, her point was simple: how could I say that I wasn't chosen after being so obviously chosen by her daughter? And how could I say that I wasn't chosen after having been welcomed so warmly into her family? And I had been. Interestingly, in family gatherings, no one had brought the whole priest thing up. I'd even been over to be vetted by the remarkable 103-year-old Ruth Dayan, Moshe's widow, in her north Tel Aviv flat. Now that visit was worth a book in itself. She said things like: 'Oh yes, I think I have a letter about that from Mr Churchill somewhere.' Anyway, I digress.

'Change the title,' said Vered. And so I did. Chosen.

7. The Sign of Jonah

The dramatic drive from Jerusalem to Jericho takes about forty minutes. At the edge of the Jerusalem suburbs the land quickly turns to mountainous, inhospitable-looking desert. A few Bedouins eke out a precarious living at the side of the road. Signs to the Good Samaritan Inn remind the traveller that it was somewhere around here that one of the most famous moral stories ever told took place, the story of a man who fell among bandits and received help, not from his fellow countrymen, but from a man he considered his enemy. Two thousand years later, the road is modern, smooth and fast, but you still wouldn't want to venture too far from the safety of an air-conditioned vehicle. Israeli forts keep a lookout from high up on the mountaintops. A sense of threat mingles with the heat. This is still a land divided into friends and enemies.

During that short journey from Jerusalem the drop is over a kilometre. At the bottom you are over a quarter of a kilometre below the level of the sea. Tens of millions of years ago, movements of the great tectonic plates forced up the land between here and what is now the Mediterranean, separating the sea from the Jordan valley. Jerusalem sits on the top. Down at the bottom, on the floor of the rift valley, it still feels a little like the seabed. The flat expanse of rocky sand, the occasional date plantation, the feeling of being exposed to some vast and empty space above – you wouldn't survive for very long out there on your own. The Dead Sea begins a few miles to the south. The Israelis call it the Salty Sea in everyday speech, but it is referred to as the Dead Sea in poetry. It contains no life – no fish or plants, hence its name. It is the lowest place on earth.

As you descend from Jerusalem, from the historic to the prehistoric, ears popping as the pressure changes, the dramatic desert cliffs of the Judaean mountains come into view to the north. This is where the dissident religious group known as the Essenes fled from the religious establishment in Jerusalem with whom they had fallen out, here to establish their own closed community of intense ascetic purity in the caves at Qumran. Discovered in the late 1940s, these caves have proved to be a treasure chest of information about first-century Judaism and those versions of the Jewish religious experience that rejected the Temple. The Essenes followed their own quasi-Messiah figure, known only as the 'Teacher of Righteousness', in a life of study and ritual cleansing, regularly washing themselves in preparation for the end of the world. It is often speculated that John the Baptist had connections with this community. Like them he emphasized the need for washing, for a baptism of repentance. The final battle was close, the kingdom of God was at hand. Here, at the edge of the world, they must get themselves ready for its final days.

But as one approaches the River Jordan itself, one is presented with signs of a much more recent conflict. In 1967 the Egyptians, the Syrians and the Jordanians were preparing to invade the State of Israel, having been opposed to its establishment from the very beginning. In anticipation of invasion, Israel struck first, destroying the Egyptian air force on the ground and sending its army deep into what had been Jordanian territory, capturing East Jerusalem, the Western Wall of the Temple, and beginning a military occupation of land that continues to this day. After the war, Israel laid down an extensive field of anti-tank and anti-personnel mines, a mile or so deep, stretching from the Dead Sea below Qumran and running for several miles north. So it was that the place traditionally understood to be the site of Jesus' baptism was cut off from the world. For decades, the only evidence of the existence of some important religious activity having occurred here was a concentration of ancient churches and monasteries, preserved intact by the lack of moisture in the air and the deadly mines in the ground.

In 2018, the Israelis began to clear the minefield as far as Qasr el-Yahud, not only the place where Jesus was reputed to have been baptized by John, but also, and not insignificantly, the place where, again by tradition, those Jews who had been led by Moses out of Egyptian slavery crossed the river with the Ark of the Covenant and so set foot in the Promised Land for the very first time. From there they made the short journey to besiege the city of Jericho, the book of Joshua famously telling the story of how its walls crumbled before the sound of the triumphant shofar. For Jews, this valley has long been of strategic importance: a buffer of sand and heat protecting Jerusalem from her enemies.

But the troubled relationship of Israel and Jordan has eased considerably since the Six Day War. These days Israeli citizens are able to travel to Jordan and many now holiday there in the south, on the Red Sea coast at Aqaba. The mine-field has lost much of its purpose, hence its decommissioning. Still, the small road down to the river presents an intimidating drive. Either side of the road fences of barbed wire separate the traveller from the remaining fields of danger, with regular signs warning of the dire consequences were one tempted to venture beyond the straight and narrow path. Past the wire, the monasteries rise up from the desert like sunken ships in a sea of death. The mines ensure an enveloping stillness. Here, in the oven of the world, nothing moves.

One day, when all the mines have gone, this place will no doubt become yet another tourist attraction on a whistle-stop tour of the Holy Land. Coaches have just started to rumble their way towards it. But many, seeking out a more eirenic-feeling baptism experience in the Holy Land still make their way to Yardenit, an undeniably beautiful site up by the Sea of Galilee that was established by an enterprising kibbutz as an alternative to Qasr el-Yahud when it became unvisitable. Following the war, those who wanted to get close to the place where Jesus was supposedly baptized did so via the Jordanian side of the river. This place, known as Bethany beyond the Jordan, is where successive popes have made their pilgrimage – John Paul II in 2000, Benedict XVI in 2009, Francis II in 2014. UNESCO declared it a World Heritage Site in 2015.

These days the water is little more than a brown trickle, the colour of the water you clean your paintbrushes in, and no more than several metres across. It remains the border between Israel and Jordan, though the only evidence of its security significance is a bored Jordanian soldier picking his teeth in the sunshine and an Israeli soldier, looking little older than a child, doing her best to look intimidating with a machine gun more than half her size.

We had decided to baptize Jonah in this place only a few days before. Lynn, myself and the boys had been staying in Tel Aviv for a few months, me trying – and mostly failing – to learn to speak Hebrew on my sabbatical. A few emails were promptly sent out to family and friends, inviting them to come. I worried that they might think it odd, all of them being Jewish and having little experience of Christianity. But they were delighted to have been asked, some even cancelling plans in order to be there. They had never seen a baptism before. Many of them had never been to that part of the Jordan either.

The only other person who might answer to the description Christian was my eldest son, Felix, who had flown out to be with us for a few days. That was rather lucky because without him the whole liturgy of baptism would not have worked, it being a highly responsorial service and, for obvious reasons, most of the congregation not being able to pledge their allegiance to Jesus, as is required. Felix also doubled as godfather. Was it odd for a congregation of Jews to gather so enthusiastically for a Christian baptism? If it was, they certainly didn't show it. Afterwards we repaired to a Christian Palestinian restaurant in Abu Ghosh for a celebratory meal. It was one of the happiest days of my life.

The dark and muddy waters of the Jordan were an invitation to cholera, someone suggested. My wife made me promise that I wouldn't submerge Jonah fully. That was fair enough. Yet Christian baptism doesn't just involve a gentle bit of water-sprinkling. It is the re-enactment of a drowning, a symbolic immersion in the death and resurrection of Jesus. The old person is drowned and the new person rises from out of the water, born again. In theological terms, this is rebirth. I was once advised to hold the child under the water a little longer than I – and certainly they might be comfortable – so that when they came up from the water they would gasp for air, as if for the first time. Like emerging from the womb. But with my own child in my arms, and my wife looking on with her 'don't you dare' face on, that was never going to happen.

Jonah's original namesake was swallowed by the great fish (not a whale, by the way) when he tried to evade God's command to go and reprimand the people of Nineveh – that city now known as Mosul, where, in 2014, ISIS terrorists had destroyed the mosque and shrine that was reputed to be his tomb. Jonah had set sail from Jaffa, the town where Lynn and I had married. But more than this personal connection, the story of Jonah had, for centuries, been appropriated by Christians as a premonition of Jesus' death and resurrection, the three days he spent in the belly of the fish being understood to be the equivalent of the three days between Jesus' death and rebirth. Down into the depths, into darkness, and then vomited up into new life. This is the so-called sign of Jonah: 'For just as Jonah was three days and three nights in the belly of the sea monster, so for three days and three nights the Son of Man will be in the heart of the earth' (Matthew 12: 40). The regurgitation of Jonah from the stomach of the fish was another one of those death-and-resurrection images.

Yet baptism is not just an initiation ceremony into the Christian club. After all, when Jesus was himself baptized at (apparently) this very spot, there was no 'in the name of the Father and the Son and the Holy Spirit' to be said – even though these words are now at the centre of the whole ceremony. Nor indeed was what John the Baptist did to Jesus at this place an induction into death and resurrection – obviously, because that hadn't happened yet. So what was its original meaning?

So many of the themes I have been exploring in this book bear down on this moment of baptism. Jesus' baptism wasn't just a baptism using water, and nor was my Jonah's. Baptism also includes anointing – marking the child's head with oil. Originally, anointing was the way in which priests and kings were consecrated for a particular purpose. The anointing of the present Queen Elizabeth at her coronation was one of the two moments (the other being the taking of Holy Communion) considered too solemn to show on television. So, as well as having echoes of drowning, baptism contains strong symbolic elements harking back to ceremonies of both ordination and coronation. The phrase 'the priesthood of all believers' is thought to have been coined by Martin Luther in the sixteenth century.

> But you are a chosen race, a royal priesthood, a holy nation, God's own people . . .
>
> (1 Peter 2:9)

In baptism, the child is drowned and crowned.

But there is also something else in the story of Jesus' own baptism that has been a central preoccupation of this book: the guiding presence of the holy spirit, the *ruach* that hovers over all creation at the beginning of time. Baptism is an investiture in creation itself. The new life is a life that is God-breathed, in the same way God breathes life into all things at the beginning of time. This is the central piece of theology that connects Christians and Jews – and indeed Muslims. It is an acknowledgement that we breathe the same air, not just life-sustaining oxygen, but also the life-sustaining breath of God. Lynn and I had received seven blessings at our marriage – another investiture harking back to the creation, as indicated by that special number. And here they were at work again.

But there can be no avoiding the divisions here, notwithstanding our shared inauguration into the blessings of creation. For as I poured the Jordan over Jonah's head, there were pilgrims doing the same thing on the other side of the river. Despite the easing of relationships, there are still Israelis who would be suspicious of 'over there'. Historically at least, it is enemy territory. We were so close I could make out a multitude of different languages wafting over the water: they were Indians and Filipinos mostly, I thought. A large group of Russians joined us on our side of the riverbank, many with terrifying tattoos all over their bodies. The baptismal candidates on both sides were being invested in a rebirth that had little time for the divisions of national boundaries. In Christ there is neither Jew nor Greek, nor Jordanian, nor Indian, nor Pole.

Nevertheless, there was still a sense of division that I was bequeathing to my son. On the one hand he is Jewish, surrounded by his Jewish and Israeli family, and – like his brother Louie – circumcised by an orthodox mohel on the eighth day of his life. He will be entitled to an Israeli passport and will be brought up speaking Hebrew. The west bank of the Jordan river is his inheritance. But with a Christian baptism, I have given him and Louie another life in solidarity with those on both sides of the river. As a priest, there was no way I could have done anything other than to desire this for my children.

Lunch was such a happy occasion that day, Jews and Christians eating and drinking together in an Arab Christian restaurant. It felt like a moment of personal healing. Of course, I am sure there will be many Jews who will be offended by the thrust of this book. They may well be disturbed by the multiple marrying outs and the marrying ins that have gone on in my family, or by what they see as my deliberate blurring of the boundaries between Christianity and Judaism. Some will be offended that Louie and Jonah have had both a bris and a baptism.

Are my wonderful boys Jewish or Christian? some may ask. Both, is all I can offer by way of answer. I am all too aware how weak this may sound to some. But in terms of their upbringing, it is our intention to bring them up as theologically bilingual. Just as they will speak both Hebrew and English, so too, I hope, they will be comfortable in both church and synagogue, at ease with the grammar of both and conversant with their ways and ceremonies. I hope this liminality will be a blessing to them, and not a source of pain. And to those who insist that they ought to renounce one side of their heritage, I can only make the obvious point that the God who hovered over creation at the beginning of time, and the God who hovered over Jesus at the River Jordan, was the same God, with the same promise.

I know that the conversion of Jews by Christians is associated with a long history of violence; conversion to Christianity being understood by both sides as a way of undoing the Jewishness of the convert. This book has been an attempt to understand the relationship between these two religions as being both more complex than this and yet also much easier. It is complex in theory – as my tortuous perambulations into Christian-Jewish theology have no doubt proved. At every stage of the argument I have been aware that there are voices objecting to what I am doing, both in terms of historical and biblical accuracy, as well as the purpose for which these arguments are being marshalled. And I have tried hard to resist the idea that there is some theoretical synthesis of Christianity and Judaism. Christianity is Christianity and Judaism is Judaism. I will always strenuously deny the idea that Christianity is some sort of upgrade of Judaism.

But as the wonderful crowd on the riverbank at Jordan that day suggested, the relationship between Jews and Christians can also be generous, joyous and supportive. Some things work better in practice than they do in theory. Would Samuel Friedeberg have approved? Certainly not the baptism bit, I'm sure of that. But perhaps he would have been content that after the break of my father marrying out, I had married back in and in some sense the continuity had been re-established, something that was torn had been repaired. Whatever he might have thought, the truth is that

I no longer seek his imagined approval. And I suppose that is why he no longer haunts me.

This book comes with a huge thank you to all those who sat around that table in Abu Ghosh, who welcomed me into their family, and who shared in the joy of that day. I hope we modelled just a little bit of ordinary, everyday *tikkun olam* – repairing the world – in the heart of land so historically disfigured by brokenness and division, especially between those of different religious traditions. Jonah means 'dove' in Hebrew. And the dove is the symbol of peace.

This book began with the unearthing of some buried personal pain and swiftly changed gear into a reflection on the inherent tension between solidarity and universality, and how this tension has run though the history of Jewish–Christian relationships. Some might think that what they have read here is two books spliced together: one a personal memoir, the other something much more theological. But, for me at least, these things are inseparable. This much I learned from Augustine. The personal is the theological and the theological is the personal. Given all these divisions, it seems appropriate that it is here, on the Jordan River, at a fault line of both political and theological geography – and literally on a fault line of the great tectonic plates – that this theological memoir comes to an end. This fault line is a crack that has run throughout my life. It is something I have learnt to live with; even, in a way, to think of as strangely precious. It's a kind of scar that accompanies my love of Judaism. It took quite a lot of psychotherapy and theological reflection to get here. And in a way, of course, I have solved nothing – there is no undoing of the historic pain that Christians have inflicted on Jews. Nor should one try. It also feels appropriate that it ends in a minefield. Throughout the course of *Chosen* I have been aware of potential mines everywhere, of the possibility of offending all sorts of people. Indeed, I'm so naturally clumsy that I'm sure I haven't avoided stepping on some of them.

I have written much of this book while sitting quietly alone in my church in south London. This place was destroyed by the Nazis on the first night of the Blitz and rebuilt after the war. The architecture is a gift to a preacher when it comes to talking about the resurrection – as, of course, was St Paul's Cathedral. But I can't help but also reflect that if it hadn't been for the bombs falling in Golders Green during the war, my father wouldn't have been evacuated to Devon as a child and then brought up among Christians. That turn of history gave me a Christian inheritance and became the basis for the way I see the world and always will do. I cannot regret it – however much the dark and disturbing thought sometimes worms around in my head that if it hadn't been for the intervention of the Luftwaffe, I probably wouldn't be a Christian.

It's not a helpful thing to dwell on. For now at least, many of my ghosts have been laid to rest. Melancholy turned to mourning – and the period of mourning has now passed. It took me seven years to work through this book. For seven years I have sat shiva, and now I am ready to begin again.

Select Bibliography

Barker, Margaret, *Temple Theology: An Introduction* (SPCK Publishing, 2004)

Berger, David, *The Rebbe, the Messiah, and the Scandal of Orthodox Indifference* (Littman Library of Jewish Civilization, 2001)

Becker, Adam and Annette Yoshiko Reed (eds), *The Ways That Never Parted: Jews and Christians in Late Antiquity and the Early Middle Ages* (pbk edn, Augsburg Fortress, 2007)

Boyarin, Daniel, *A Radical Jew: Paul and the Politics of Identity* (University of California Press, 1994)

—, *Border Lines: The Partition of Judaeo-Christianity* (University of Pennsylvania Press, 2004)

—, *The Jewish Gospels: The Story of the Jewish Christ* (The New Press, 2012)

—, *Judaism: The Genealogy of a Modern Notion* (Rutgers University Press, 2019)

Brueggemann, Walter, *The Prophetic Imagination* (Fortress Press, 2001)

—, *Chosen? Reading the Bible amid the Israeli-Palestinian Conflict* (Westminster John Knox Press, 2015)

Cohen, Shaye J. D., *From the Maccabees to the Mishnah* (Westminster John Knox Press, 1987)

—., *The Beginnings of Jewishness: Boundaries, Varieties, Uncertainties* (University of California Press, 1999)

Cohn, Haim, *The Trial and Death of Jesus* (Harper & Row, 1971)

Douglas, Mary, *Leviticus as Literature* (Oxford University Press, 1999)

Fraser, Giles, *Christianity with Attitude* (Canterbury Press, 2007)

Frosh, Stephen, *Hauntings: Psychoanalysis and Ghostly Transmissions* (Palgrave Macmillan, 2013)

Goldhill, Simon, *The Temple of Jerusalem* (Harvard University Press, 2011)

Goodman, Martin, *A History of Judaism* (Allen Lane, 2017)

Haidt, Jonathan, *The Righteous Mind: Why Good People are Divided by Politics and Religion* (Penguin, 2012)

Heilman, Samuel and Menachem Friedman, *The Rebbe: The Life and Afterlife of Menachem Mendel Schneerson* (Princeton University Press, 2010)

Klawans, Jonathan, *Impurity and Sin in Ancient Judaism* (Oxford University Press, 2000)

—, *Purity, Sacrifice, and the Temple: Symbolism and Supersessionism in the Study of Ancient Judaism* (Oxford University Press, 2006)

Kundera, Milan, *The Unbearable Lightness of Being* (Harper & Row, 1984)

Kushner, Tony, *Anglo-Jewry since 1066: Place, Locality and Memory* (Manchester University Press, 2009)

Phillips, Adam, *On Balance* (Farrar Straus Giroux, 2010)

—, *Becoming Freud: The Making of a Psychoanalyst* (Yale University Press, 2014)

Rose, Gillian, *Mourning Becomes the Law: Philosophy and Representation* (Cambridge University Press, 1996)

Tec, Nechama, *In the Lion's Den: The Life of Oswald Rufeisen* (Oxford University Press, 1990)

Williams, Rowan, *Silence and Honey Cakes: The Wisdom of the Desert* (Lion Hudson, 2003)

Acknowledgements

This book has taken far too long to write, and has tested the patience of many who have supported me. A massive thank you goes especially to Simon Winder, my publisher at Penguin, for his kindly and intelligent presence throughout, and also to Sarah Chalfant at the Wylie Agency for always being in my corner, and always with such strong advice.

A number of people have helped me with this project along the way, either with conversations about its subject matter, or having read and commented on various drafts of the manuscript. Josh Cohen was the most generous reader, saving me from several howlers. Thanks also to Geoffrey Alderman (I resisted his tempting suggestion I should include dis-acknowledgements as well as acknowledgements), and to Harvey Belowski, Stephen Frosh, Maurice Glasman, Tom Holland, Laura Janner-Klausner, William Kolbrener, David Lan, Jonathan Romain, Jane Steen, Vered Tandler-Dayan, Gordon Wassermann and Rowan Williams. Also, thanks to the brilliant Adam Phillips for guiding me in the early stages to think more carefully about Freud and religion. Needless to say, all the mistakes and controversial opinions contained here are mine, not theirs – and many of them because I have ignored their good counsel.

I also want to thank my wonderful children, Alice, Isabella, Felix, Louie and Jonah for being my reason to live. They are my life and purpose, and I adore them more than I can say. Thanks also to the congregation of the church of St Mary, Newington, in south London, where I have the privilege to serve as their parish priest. Their prayers have supported me throughout the writing of this book.

I also want to offer a very special thank you to Rabbi Lord Sacks, of blessed memory. In his eulogy for Rabbi Sacks at his funeral, my friend Rabbi Belovski, speaking of how Rabbi Sacks was able to influence such a wide variety of people, made reference to a very special Shabbat dinner that he hosted just before lockdown. 'Giles and Lynn ate a while ago with Jonathan and Elaine at our home,' he recalled 'And you may remember [Rabbi Sacks] dancing with his children – Giles has Jewish children with a Jewish wife – and this has absolutely transformed the way they are bringing up their children to give them a Jewish content in their lives. Extraordinary.' And it's true. Rabbi Sacks has been a huge influence. 'And although we argued – he really didn't like my interpretation of Daniel 7, and was understandably nervous about my use of the Rebbe (who had made such a dramatic and personal difference within his own life) – he was always generous and respectful in his conversations with me, and I always came away from them a different person.

But it is to two women that I dedicate this book, both of whom saved my life.

To Susie Orbach, I will never be able to thank you enough for allowing me to fall apart on your sofa, for being a light in the darkness, and for helping me to recognize the difference between plain unhappiness and catastrophe.

But most of all to Lynn Tandler, my wife and my love. Without her this book would not have happened, and the reconstruction it describes could not have taken place. She chose me and pulled me back from the edge. This book may be a kind of ghost story – but it is mostly a love story. And the title of this book is an expression of my gratitude to her.

The baptism of Jonah Boris Tandler Fraser
The River Jordan, October 2019

ALLEN LANE
an imprint of
PENGUIN BOOKS

Also Published

Emma Smith, *Portable Magic: A History of Books and their Readers*

Kris Manjapra, *Black Ghost of Empire: The Long Death of Slavery and the Failure of Emancipation*

Andrew Scull, *Desperate Remedies: Psychiatry and the Mysteries of Mental Illness*

James Bridle, *Ways of Being: Beyond Human Intelligence*

Eugene Linden, *Fire and Flood: A People's History of Climate Change, from 1979 to the Present*

Cathy O'Neil, *The Shame Machine: Who Profits in the New Age of Humiliation*

Peter Hennessy, *A Duty of Care: Britain Before and After Covid*

Gerd Gigerenzer, *How to Stay Smart in a Smart World: Why Human Intelligence Still Beats Algorithms*

Halik Kochanski, *Resistance: The Undergroud War in Europe, 1939-1945*

Joseph Sassoon, *The Global Merchants: The Enterprise and Extravagance of the Sassoon Dynasty*

Clare Chambers, *Intact: A Defence of the Unmodified Body*

Nina Power, *What Do Men Want?: Masculinity and Its Discontents*

Ivan Jablonka, *A History of Masculinity: From Patriarchy to Gender Justice*

Thomas Halliday, *Otherlands: A World in the Making*

Sofi Thanhauser, *Worn: A People's History of Clothing*

Sebastian Mallaby, *The Power Law: Venture Capital and the Art of Disruption*

David J. Chalmers, *Reality+: Virtual Worlds and the Problems of Philosophy*

Jing Tsu, *Kingdom of Characters: A Tale of Language, Obsession and Genius in Modern China*

Lewis R. Gordon, *Fear of Black Consciousness*

Leonard Mlodinow, *Emotional: The New Thinking About Feelings*

Kevin Birmingham, *The Sinner and the Saint: Dostoevsky, a Crime and Its Punishment*

Roberto Calasso, *The Book of All Books*

Marit Kapla, *Osebol: Voices from a Swedish Village*

Malcolm Gaskill, *The Ruin of All Witches: Life and Death in the New World*

Mark Mazower, *The Greek Revolution: 1821 and the Making of Modern Europe*

Paul McCartney, *The Lyrics: 1956 to the Present*

Brendan Simms and Charlie Laderman, *Hitler's American Gamble: Pearl Harbor and the German March to Global War*

Lea Ypi, *Free: Coming of Age at the End of History*

David Graeber and David Wengrow, *The Dawn of Everything: A New History of Humanity*

Ananyo Bhattacharya, *The Man from the Future: The Visionary Life of John von Neumann*

Andrew Roberts, *George III: The Life and Reign of Britain's Most Misunderstood Monarch*

James Fox, *The World According to Colour: A Cultural History*

Clare Jackson, *Devil-Land: England Under Siege, 1588-1688*

Steven Pinker, *Rationality: Why It Is, Why It Seems Scarce, Why It Matters*

Volker Ullrich, *Eight Days in May: How Germany's War Ended*

Adam Tooze, *Shutdown: How Covide Shook the World's Economy*

Tristram Hunt, *The Radical Potter: Josiah Wedgwood and the Transformation of Britain*

Paul Davies, *What's Eating the Universe: And Other Cosmic Questions*

Shon Faye, *The Transgender Issue: An Argument for Justice*

Dennis Duncan, *Index, A History of the*

Richard Overy, *Blood and Ruins: The Great Imperial War, 1931-1945*

Paul Mason, *How to Stop Fascism: History, Ideology, Resistance*

Cass R. Sunstein and Richard H. Thaler, *Nudge: Improving Decisions About Health, Wealth and Happiness*

Lisa Miller, *The Awakened Brain: The Psychology of Spirituality and Our Search for Meaning*

Michael Pye, *Antwerp: The Glory Years*

Christopher Clark, *Prisoners of Time: Prussians, Germans and Other Humans*

Rupa Marya and Raj Patel, *Inflamed: Deep Medicine and the Anatomy of Injustice*

Richard Zenith, *Pessoa: An Experimental Life*

Michael Pollan, *This Is Your Mind On Plants: Opium—Caffeine—Mescaline*

Amartya Sen, *Home in the World: A Memoir*

Jan-Werner Müller, *Democracy Rules*

Robin DiAngelo, *Nice Racism: How Progressive White People Perpetuate Racial Harm*

Rosemary Hill, *Time's Witness: History in the Age of Romanticism*

Lawrence Wright, *The Plague Year: America in the Time of Covid*

Adrian Wooldridge, *The Aristocracy of Talent: How Meritocracy Made the Modern World*

Julian Hoppit, *The Dreadful Monster and its Poor Relations: Taxing, Spending and the United Kingdom, 1707-2021*

Jordan Ellenberg, *Shape: The Hidden Geometry of Absolutely Everything*

Duncan Campbell-Smith, *Crossing Continents: A History of Standard Chartered Bank*

Jemma Wadham, *Ice Rivers*

Niall Ferguson, *Doom: The Politics of Catastrophe*

Michael Lewis, *The Premonition: A Pandemic Story*

Chiara Marletto, *The Science of Can and Can't: A Physicist's Journey Through the Land of Counterfactuals*

Suzanne Simard, *Finding the Mother Tree: Uncovering the Wisdom and Intelligence of the Forest*

Giles Fraser, *Chosen: Lost and Found between Christianity and Judaism*

Malcolm Gladwell, *The Bomber Mafia: A Story Set in War*

Kate Darling, *The New Breed: How to Think About Robots*

Serhii Plokhy, *Nuclear Folly: A New History of the Cuban Missile Crisis*

Sean McMeekin, *Stalin's War*

Michio Kaku, *The God Equation: The Quest for a Theory of Everything*

Michael Barber, *Accomplishment: How to Achieve Ambitious and Challenging Things*

Charles Townshend, *The Partition: Ireland Divided, 1885-1925*

Hanif Abdurraqib, *A Little Devil in America: In Priase of Black Performance*

Carlo Rovelli, *Helgoland*

Herman Pontzer, *Burn: The Misunderstood Science of Metabolism*

Jordan B. Peterson, *Beyond Order: 12 More Rules for Life*

Bill Gates, *How to Avoid a Climate Disaster: The Solutions We Have and the Breakthroughs We Need*

Kehinde Andrews, *The New Age of Empire: How Racism and Colonialism Still Rule the World*

Veronica O'Keane, *The Rag and Bone Shop: How We Make Memories and Memories Make Us*

Robert Tombs, *This Sovereign Isle: Britain In and Out of Europe*

Mariana Mazzucato, *Mission Economy: A Moonshot Guide to Changing Capitalism*

Frank Wilczek, *Fundamentals: Ten Keys to Reality*

Milo Beckman, *Math Without Numbers*

John Sellars, *The Fourfold Remedy: Epicurus and the Art of Happiness*

T. G. Otte, *Statesman of Europe: A Life of Sir Edward Grey*

Alex Kerr, *Finding the Heart Sutra: Guided by a Magician, an Art Collector and Buddhist Sages from Tibet to Japan*

Edwin Gale, *The Species That Changed Itself: How Prosperity Reshaped Humanity*

Simon Baron-Cohen, *The Pattern Seekers: A New Theory of Human Invention*

Christopher Harding, *The Japanese: A History of Twenty Lives*

Carlo Rovelli, *There Are Places in the World Where Rules Are Less Important Than Kindness*

Ritchie Robertson, *The Enlightenment: The Pursuit of Happiness 1680-1790*

Ivan Krastev, *Is It Tomorrow Yet?: Paradoxes of the Pandemic*

Tim Harper, *Underground Asia: Global Revolutionaries and the Assault on Empire*

John Gray, *Feline Philosophy: Cats and the Meaning of Life*

Priya Satia, *Time's Monster: History, Conscience and Britain's Empire*

Fareed Zakaria, *Ten Lessons for a Post-Pandemic World*

David Sumpter, *The Ten Equations that Rule the World: And How You Can Use Them Too*

Richard J. Evans, *The Hitler Conspiracies: The Third Reich and the Paranoid Imagination*

Fernando Cervantes, *Conquistadores*

John Darwin, *Unlocking the World: Port Cities and Globalization in the Age of Steam, 1830-1930*

Michael Strevens, *The Knowledge Machine: How an Unreasonable Idea Created Modern Science*

Owen Jones, *This Land: The Story of a Movement*

Seb Falk, *The Light Ages: A Medieval Journey of Discovery*

Daniel Yergin, *The New Map: Energy, Climate, and the Clash of Nations*

Michael J. Sandel, *The Tyranny of Merit: What's Become of the Common Good?*

Joseph Henrich, *The Weirdest People in the World: How the West Became Psychologically Peculiar and Particularly Prosperous*

Leonard Mlodinow, *Stephen Hawking: A Memoir of Friendship and Physics*

David Goodhart, *Head Hand Heart: The Struggle for Dignity and Status in the 21st Century*

Claudia Rankine, *Just Us: An American Conversation*

James Rebanks, *English Pastoral: An Inheritance*

Robin Lane Fox, *The Invention of Medicine: From Homer to Hippocrates*

Daniel Lieberman, *Exercised: The Science of Physical Activity, Rest and Health*

Sudhir Hazareesingh, *Black Spartacus: The Epic Life of Touissaint Louverture*